WORDS ON W__

Memories of the 'Home Front' during the Second World War
from the people of the Kirklees area

HELGA HUGHES

"WELL, ALFIE, HOW DO YOU LIKE THE NEW BABY!"
"HE LOOKS ALRIGHT, MOM—**HOW MANY COUPONS?**"

A "BAMFORTH" COMIC

KIRKLEES SOUND ARCHIVE

ISBN 0 900746 42 4

Kirklees Metropolitan Council
Cultural Services
Red Doles Lane
Huddersfield
HD2 1YF

Technical and Commercial Unit
Oakwell Hall
Nutter Lane
Birstall
Batley
WF17 9LG

Designed and Typeset by
Arrunden Associates

Printed by Titus Wilson & Son,
Burneside Road, Kendal
on Printsetter Velvet 130gm²

CONTENTS

ACKNOWLEDGEMENTS

My acknowledgements and thanks go to the following individuals and organizations:

First and foremost to all the local people who gave their memories of life during the Second World War to Kirklees Sound Archive and made this publication possible. (From its outset the policy of Kirklees Sound Archive has been to guarantee anonymity to all interviewees, and therefore the names of those who contributed their memories cannot be listed).

To all the Kirklees Sound Archive staff over the years, whose work has helped to create such a unique archive of local history, and to Katherine Towsey, Assistant Curator (Oral History).

To Bamforth & Co. Ltd. of Holmfirth for their kind permission to reproduce their wartime postcards in this publication.

To the following local people for their kind permission to use their personal photographs, ephemera and wartime artefacts in this book:
Mrs B Battye, Mr P H Bell, Mrs M Bowers, Mrs M Garner, Mrs H Gibson, Miss V Gill, Mr E Hepworth, Mrs E L Holroyd, Mrs J Hudson, Mrs A Hurst, Mrs B Johnson, Ms A Mackintosh, Mr C H Smith, Mrs E Wragg.

To the following local newspapers for their kind permission to include illustrations and news articles from their wartime editions:
The Reporter Group
The Huddersfield Daily Examiner
Spenborough Guardian

To Jane Helliwell of Huddersfield Local Studies Library for her assistance in accessing the Bamforth postcard collection.

To M R Hepworth for research and editorial assistance.

To Elizabeth Hayes and George Jackson for photography.

To Joanne Gascoigne, Isobel Schofield and Grace Wood of the Kirklees Technical and Commercial Unit for production, editorial and typing support.

INTRODUCTION - THE PEOPLE'S WAR

The Second World War affected, to varying degrees, life for everyone in Britain. Those conscripted into the Armed Forces experienced a total change from civilian life, but this was not a war confined only to the Armed Forces - it was a war that also involved every civilian. Many faced traumatic experiences and even death as they suffered enemy air attacks, and everyone was subject to the Government's necessary control over people and resources under wartime conditions.

Kirklees was fortunate not to suffer major bombing, death and destruction like some areas of Britain. However, everyone had to endure the everyday difficulties and requirements of wartime life. Local people experienced loneliness and worry as loved ones were called up; the inconvenient and dangerous darkness of the black-out; the dash for shelter as the siren sounded; the fear and uncertainty as German aeroplanes flew overhead. They coped with rationing, shortages and the endless queueing for goods; worked in our vital war industries or outside the area in mining, munitions or the Land Army; knitted woollens for the Forces and contributed to the massive amounts saved and salvaged locally for the war effort; and opened their homes to evacuees and refugees. Hundreds of local men volunteered to defend their country in the Home Guard, and men and women daily undertook often arduous Civil Defence duties. For those who lived through the war, these years provided some of the most memorable experiences of their lives.

This book reveals something of life on the 'Home Front' during the war in the words of local people who lived through it. It will recall memories for those who were there at the time, and inform those who were not, about everyday life for ordinary men, women and children.

We can obtain an interpretation of the war from National and Local Government records, statistics and other conventional historical sources. Factual information relating to wartime life is readily available. But how did people feel? How did they relate to the facts? What was everyday life really like? In Kirklees, people were asked to remember. Oral history reveals the local and personal real life incidents and feelings not recorded in the national historical record - the 'flesh on the bones' of historical fact. It captures the struggle against cold and shortages, the loss of loved ones, the fear of death or injury, the long hours at work: the humour, the sadness, the joy, the grief, the envy and the sharing.

Postcards highlighting wartime themes produced locally by Bamforth & Co. of Holmfirth help to illustrate this book, as do extracts from local newspapers which, although censored, could still report on the daily concerns of a people at war. Government information leaflets have been saved for half a century in the homes of the people who received them, along with telegrams and greetings from loved ones away on Active Service, badges and certificates of those who served in the Home Guard or ARP, the gas masks and cookery books which were once in everyday use. These, together with personal photographs kept for all those years in the albums of local people, have helped to piece together a picture of life as it was lived by the people of Kirklees on the Home Front.

There is no single story of life on the Home Front. There were indeed many common experiences, but these memories also reveal something of the immense gulf that could lie between people, even those in apparently similar situations, who express different interpretations, attitudes and feelings. For many wartime was a time of hardship and deprivation; for some, who could afford the price or knew the right people, most things were available. Memories show how systems such as rationing although intended to be fair were, in reality, not. Some obtained more than their share, and others were too poor to take their proper share. National campaigns urged against 'squandering' money or wasting fuel and food, yet for many people conservation was already a way of life, and there was nothing to squander.

For many, war had a devastating effect of upheaval, loneliness and bereavement; whilst for others it was a time of excitement, adventure and independence. Whatever their experiences, for many local people the war years appear to have been one of the most extraordinary times of their lives, in many cases changing the whole course of their lives, and creating memories which would endure.

NOTE: The term 'Kirklees' is used in this book though the author acknowledges that this Local Authority administrative area did not exist until 1974. It indicates that the material in this book relates to the area now encompassed within the present boundaries of Kirklees.

Helga Hughes
*Community Curator, Red House, Gomersal
(former Sound Archivist, Kirklees Museums).*

THE INTERVIEWS

Kirklees Sound Archive, part of Kirklees Cultural Services, was established in 1985 with the aim of recording the memories of the people of Kirklees on tape in order to build up an oral history archive of the Kirklees area and its inhabitants. Photographs and documents relating to the oral history interviews are also collected and copied. The Archive now contains over 600 interviews of Kirklees people telling their own history in their own words, and provides a unique source of information on many aspects of twentieth century life in this area.

The quotations in this book are taken from around 100 oral history interviews in the Wartime, Childhood and Industry project sections of the Kirklees Sound Archive. These interviews were designed to cover a broad range of wartime experiences and situations on the Home Front during the Second World War. They include those people who were children and those who were too old to go to war; those in reserved occupations and Bevin Boys; workers in our major industries of textiles, engineering and chemicals; housewives and women conscripted to the Forces, the Land Army or munitions.

There are interviews with ARP Wardens, Home Guard, police, nurses, ambulance and first aid workers; local children and incoming evacuees; wealthy and poor; those who suffered great sacrifices and those who were relatively little affected. All these local people contributed their personal histories to this unique archive of memories of life on the Home Front.

These extracts form only a small part of the vast and continually growing collection of memories in the Kirklees Sound Archive. The full collections of the Archive are available to the public in the Local Studies section of Huddersfield Central Library.

THE POSTCARDS

We are fortunate to have within the Kirklees area the firm of Bamforth & Co. Ltd. of Holmfirth, who produced all the postcards illustrated in this book. In 1870 James Bamforth, a keen photographer, opened his own photographic portrait studio in Holmfirth. He then successfully moved into lantern slide production and film making. In 1904 the Company began producing postcards, which had become the predominant form of communication, used much as the telephone is today. During the First World War Bamforth's produced great quantities of mainly sentimental postcards.

Bamforth postcards of the Second World War, in contrast to those of the First World War, are mostly comic, although some sentimental ones were produced. Their very popular cards illustrated almost every aspect of life on the Home Front, providing a humorous viewpoint on the many hardships suffered by the civilian population in Britain.

Many of the themes of the postcards echo the memories of local people. Shortages of food and other goods such as bananas, petrol and stockings are a recurring concern in both oral history interviews and postcards. The various Civil Defence roles undertaken by civilians provided popular targets for a joke. The many cards ridiculing Hitler provided a way for people to express their feelings. Cards depicting women's role in munitions and the Land Army, although humorous, acknowledged their skills and hard work. It is interesting to note that cards reflecting the hope for a better and more socially just future after the war were popular long before its end was in sight.

THE FIRST DAY ...

On the September weekend that war was declared, many Kirklees people were enjoying their summer holidays at the seaside. The war came as no surprise however, and long before Neville Chamberlain's announcement at 11.15 a.m. on Sunday 3rd September 1939 that Britain was at war with Germany, the Kirklees area, in common with the rest of the country, had begun its preparations for war. Gas masks had been issued, and precautions against air raids were under way with the erection of shelters and recruitment of Civil Defence personnel.

That first night the air raid warning siren sounded, causing apprehension and some indignation amongst local people. It tested the newly formed local emergency services, who performed well according to the local press. The Chief Fire Officer in Batley stated he had 'never seen men report for duty so quickly'. The press also reported on large numbers of people who gathered in the streets when the alarm was given. A letter in *The Huddersfield Examiner* described how light after light came on in bedrooms, despite the fact that the black-out had been in force for three nights. Fortunately it was only a false alarm, but although it was to be many months before the war really took effect, it was a taste of what was to come for those at home.

Many local people clearly recall that day and all the emotion that the prospect of war caused in their homes. Few realised then how long the war would last.

"We were expecting the announcement on the radio and we were all there in the living room, sitting there listening to it, and mother started to cry, and father who'd been in the First World War was very upset at the thought of any of his children having to go. I always remember him saying 'I'd give my right arm rather than have any of you go through what I did in the First World War'. It was a very emotional occasion of course."
HUDDERSFIELD WOMAN BORN 1923

"The Sunday morning when the broadcast was on announcing that we were all at war, I can remember coming in and my mother was crying, heartbroken, really sobbing, and I had never seen my mother sob like that before, I can remember that really well."
CLECKHEATON WOMAN BORN 1932

"I didn't take it too seriously because not knowing what war was like, not knowing how serious it could be, I think I was pleased. It's a shame to say so now but I think at the time I was pleased. I was thrilled ... I thought a few weeks it'd be all over."
GOLCAR MAN BORN 1922

"I was in a caravan in Scarborough with my wife's parents, before we were married, and we heard the news over the radio and straight away we thought things were going to start cracking y'know and we packed up and came home. And of course nothing happened for nine months after that."
HOLMFIRTH MAN BORN 1910

"... the first night the sirens went at two o'clock in the morning and we all got up and we thought 'By jingoes, they've soon got here have the Germans!' - and everybody congregated at the top of our yard."
KIRKHEATON WOMAN BORN 1921

GOSH! I WISH I'D ONE O' THEM DICTATORS HERE... JUST FOR TWO MINUTES!

THE FIRST DAY ...

"We were in Blackpool for a holiday and on the Friday night we went to the circus, and when we came out everything was black, every light had been turned off ... so we'd a job getting home. And I spent all the next day going round Blackpool buying black-out curtain materials and then when we came home on Sunday we spent the whole day putting up curtains, black curtains all over. And about eight o'clock at night we had the glass door to do in the front. We were just doing that and a Warden shouted 'Put that light out!' so that was the beginning."
HUDDERSFIELD WOMAN BORN 1899

My father forced us to go into the shelter the first night that the war started. There wasn't a raid but there was a warning. And he swore - he says 'The buggers are 'ere'. Anyway, we had to go into the shelter - me father, mother, two brothers and myself - all wearing gas masks! And everything was serious, very very serious. I looked at me mother, me mother looked at me - we were both great gigglers - tears ran down my face - and you can imagine what its like trying to giggle in a gas mask, they kept blowing [makes rude noises]. My father said if we couldn't take it serious we might as well get out!"
GOLCAR MAN BORN 1922

"Two o'clock in the morning the sirens went for the first time and we all rushed into the cellar, and I went into the coal cellar - and I found my nightie in there the next morning 'cause we'd to dress down the stairs. And we sat there till daylight, and I said 'Oh good gracious there's nothing going on' and we came up. And there was a man passing and I said 'Are the sirens over?'. 'Oh' he says 'get back to your bed, they've been over long since!'."
HUDDERSFIELD WOMAN BORN 1899

LEND A HAND ON THE LAND

SAVE WASTE PAPER

LEND TO DEFEND

PUT THAT LIGHT OUT

ALWAYS CARRY YOUR GAS MASK

From that first day the life of every citizen was subject to the instructions and exhortations of the Government as the demands of war enveloped the country.

WHAT TO DO ABOUT GAS

DIG FOR VICTORY

KEEP IT DARK

IF THE INVADER COMES

CARELESS TALK COSTS LIVES

INTO DARKNESS

One of the worst aspects of the war for many local people was the almost total 'black-out' of all homes, streets, public buildings and transport in order to help prevent enemy air attack after nightfall. The black-out caused many practical difficulties for people, and was also highly dangerous in itself with many injuries and deaths resulting from car crashes, falls, and other accidents in the darkness. The effects of enemy bombing varied greatly around the country, but everyone suffered from the black-out.

ANOTHER BLACK-OUT TRAGEDY
VOICE: "LOOK QUICK AND COME TO BED, ALFRED!"
MAN "HECK --- WHERE AM I? THEY DON'T CALL ME ALFRED!"

"... terrible, because as I say we had no lights at all. We had no lights - you just had to guess, an' if you knew your road it wasn't so bad, but if you didn't know your road you were lost ..."
HUDDERSFIELD WOMAN BORN 1910

"... at first when you went out into it, being used to lamps, even gas lamps ... something to guide you, something to go by, it was very difficult - at first. But when you'd been out a few hours you could see a little bit, you could see the general outline of things, particularly if it was moonlight. I think the moonlight was a bigger danger than leaking lights from black-outs."
GOLCAR MAN BORN 1922

"Lots of people had accidents - walking into lamp-posts, being run over ..."
HUDDERSFIELD WOMAN BORN 1925

"Me dad died in 1942 ... he was only ill three days, and he'd fallen in the black-out and he'd hurt his leg. Well you'd have thought it was nothing ... [the doctor] says 'Oh he's got a touch of flu and the fall has knocked him a bit out, but I think a few days in bed and he'll be all right' ..."
HUDDERSFIELD WOMAN BORN 1902

"The buses were very dimly lit inside and outside. Inside the windows were a dark blue, and they also carried on the windows a kind of a mesh which was there to stop shrapnel or anything like that ... and it was very difficult to see your destination. If you didn't know by the bumps in the road where you were, you'd gone past!"
GOLCAR MAN BORN 1922

FATAL COLLISION IN "BLACK-OUT."

Mirfield Mine Worker Killed.

Dewsbury's First "Black-Out" Victim.

It is to be hoped that the public will take heed of the advice to keep off the roads during the hours of darkness, made by the District Coroner, Mr. C. J. Haworth, at an inquest on Dewsbury's first victim of the "black-out" regulations. Mr. Haworth said such fatalities were occurring up and down the country, and showed how essential it was that people should exercise every possible care.

The Coroner was investigating the death of a Dewsbury builder's labourer who came into contact with a 'bus in Halifax Road, Dewsbury, shortly before ten o'clock on Monday night. He was killed immediately and the evidence showed that in the darkness the driver never saw the man cross the road.

Many pedestrians are wearing white armlets as a precaution.

FELL THROUGH ROOF WHILE "BLACKING-OUT."

Inquest on Painter.

"The stations were not illuminated, or illuminated very very badly ... You couldn't really tell which station you was at sometimes until you were actually on the platform and you'd shout at the porter 'Where are we?'."
HUDDERSFIELD MAN BORN 1931

"It were absolute chaos wa' t'black-out, and all ever t'motor cars had at t'front ... you took yer headlamp glass out and put these here [covers] in, and all they wa', there were about four or five slits, and it wa' facing down. You could just see a bit o' summat at t'front. You couldn't see nowt from up above. Ah, it were a devil. It were a rough do wa' t'black-out."
ROBERTTOWN MAN BORN 1912

"All kinds of things sprouted. The edges of kerbs, kerbstones were painted white, the running boards of cars were painted white, and the wings."
BATLEY MAN BORN 1926

Car headlamp mask. These were made compulsory in 1940. The light shone downwards through the horizontal slits.

LOOK, FIDO, THEY'VE DECORATED FOR US!

ENGLAND EXPECTS EVERY MAN THIS NIGHT TO DO HIS DUTY!

IT'S AFTER BLACKOUT TIME I SUPPOSE WE OUGHT TO TELL HER!

AIR WARD

Not even the smallest chink of light was supposed to show from doors and windows. Curtains, blinds, or thick brown paper screens were common methods of 'blacking out' homes. It was the ARP Warden's job to ensure that the black-out regulations were carried out. Offenders could be taken to court and fined, and many cases were reported in the local newspapers. A Huddersfield farmer was 'fined £5 for displaying a light from a cowshed during black-out' - it was his fourth conviction for similar offences! Most local people though appear to have been very conscientious about the effectiveness of their black-out.

"... when you drew your black-out curtains one of you was sent outside - 'Have a look and see if you can see any light' - and you knew then you were all right."
HUDDERSFIELD MAN BORN 1924

"Well we used to have to go and knock on t'doors and t'windows and tell 'em to 'Put that light out' you see. Even if they lit a cigarette up you'd to go and tell 'em to put it out. You hadn't to show a spark at all, because they could see it from t'air."
LIVERSEDGE WOMAN BORN 1910
ARP WARDEN

"Early on in the Home Guard days, when we were on the observation post ... there was a farm just across the road ... the farmer had a light in his yard, and he would have this blessed thing on in the middle of the night, never mind just after black-out time. And he'd been warned by the ARP people and our lads had been down to tell him - you know, 'Better get this out', and he wasn't very co-operative. And one of our chaps said 'I'll cure that blighter' ... one night this chap whipped up his rifle and took a pot shot at the light. And there was a devil to do about that but it cured that farmer. He kept his light out after that."
HIGHTOWN MAN BORN 1920
HOME GUARD

INTO DARKNESS

Quite apart from the physical accidents caused by the darkness, the question of whether it was safe to be out in the black-out causes some differences of opinion amongst local people.

"It was horrible, yes, hated it. It was awful. We always had a torch with us, everybody had a torch, and if you went to a dance you took each other home. You know, a gang of us we'd take Jean home 'cause she lived further over ... and when I had a boyfriend my mum used to come and meet me when he had gone home on the bus 'cause she wouldn't let us go home in the dark. It was scary ... I was scared of the black-out, I really was."
HECKMONDWIKE WOMAN BORN 1926

BOY SHOPBREAKERS CAUGHT.

" Black-Out " Robberies.

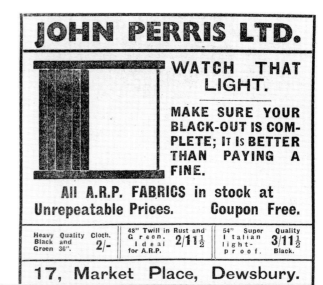

THISH BLACK-OUT'SH AN ABSHOLUTE SUCCESS... CAN'T SEE A THING, ALFRED!

Shop Early.
Dewsbury Open Market will be closed at sunset, in order to comply with the lighting restrictions. Do your shopping early.

"Well, we used to have badges that we bought, and they were luminous, they didn't shine as a torch but you could tell if someone was coming towards you. And also we had torches which we used to keep [directed] on the ground. Actually I think if I could take my pick, I'd live through the black-out days again rather than today because we were a damned sight safer in the black-out than what they are today."
HUDDERSFIELD WOMAN BORN 1924

"I remember one morning, coming home about two o'clock in the morning, and I heard these heavy footsteps coming towards me and I thought, 'Oh it's another Warden coming off duty from the other post' and just as we got by each other I said, 'Friend or foe?'. He says, 'I can be either!' I nearly died. I never ran so fast in all my life."
DEWSBURY WOMAN BORN 1897
ARP WARDEN

"It was very dark and no lights of course but yet I never heard ever of anyone being mugged or robbed or anything of that sort. We never knew anything of anything like that. But we did used to go about. We used to go dancing, I know we came up from a dance and the post office van picked us up to give us a lift up to Birkenshaw and he nearly ran into a roundabout. And we'd have been in trouble if the police had caught us if he had hit that roundabout, because it was illegal to carry anyone in a mail van."
HIGHTOWN WOMAN BORN 1919

WHEN THE SIRENS WENT

There was a great fear of large-scale air attack from Germany, and Kirklees was prepared for the possibility of heavy air raids. As well as the general air raid precautions, the local population was issued with instructions on 'What to do in an Air Raid' and how to cope if they were bombed out of their homes. Emergency feeding and rest centres were established around the district, as well as first aid posts to deal with minor injuries. Although actual air raids turned out to be few in Kirklees, there were a great many air raid warnings as German aeroplanes flew overhead night after night to bomb cities such as Manchester and Liverpool. For local people there was always the fear that they could be 'next'.

"The very sound of the siren struck a fear into you. I mean, as soon as that siren went I can remember me heart pounding and I'd listen - you could tell which were German planes y'know and which were English by the sound of them. And you'd be listening and me mother'd be saying 'Come on, come down, get dressed, come down' and we'd all go into the cellar and sit under the cellar steps - sometimes all night y'know until the sirens went."
HUDDERSFIELD WOMAN BORN 1925

"It was scary yes, because now you hear a plane and it goes 'Zoom' and in those days they just went over steady, nearly like a car going up the road, just went over steady. And you could hear them heavy ladened, droning - just going 'Drone'. And me dad always used to say 'Oh they're coming back, they've dropped their bombs' but we knew - we were kids, but we knew they were heavy. And we could tell when they were going over they were heavy with bombs, and we knew when they came back they weren't ... I never got used to them, I never got used to that. We got used to a lot of things but I didn't used to like it when the aeroplanes went over - I was scared. All of us were scared."
HECKMONDWIKE WOMAN BORN 1926

WHO WANTS BLINKING SEARCHLIGHTS TO-NIGHT?

"I know we used to be terrified. We used to say 'Oh there's a full moon tonight, they'll come'."
DEWSBURY WOMAN BORN 1897

"It got to the point we didn't bother getting up when the sirens went, here in Huddersfield. You got sort of immune to it. Sometimes it was a couple of times a night y'know - the 'All Clear' would go, you'd get back into bed and then it'd start again - you got up again, y'know, two or three times a night. I mean you were pretty weary sometimes, so that's why eventually you got till you preferred your sleep."
HUDDERSFIELD WOMAN BORN 1915

"... there were many a night when German bombers came over and they passed over - this was the main route to such places as Liverpool and Manchester, so I mean to say it was almost every night during the winter of 1940 they were coming over - just a simple drone all the time ... but strangely enough we got used to it, and as that winter went on we got to taking no notice - it was just a drone. Until one evening somebody, one of them dropped a land mine by the Town Hall in Dewsbury, just above the Town Hall in Dewsbury, Wakefield Road - and that wakened us all up a little bit you know!"
MIRFIELD MAN BORN 1922

AIR RAIDS

Sometimes the German bombers did not just pass over Kirklees. This area did not suffer from bombing to anything like the same extent as places such as London, Coventry or Hull, and many local people recall how fortunate we were - some of them could even see and hear the bombing of Sheffield, Leeds and Bradford. However, high explosive bombs, land mines and incendiaries did fall in various areas of Kirklees, mainly between August 1940 and summer 1941, the period of the German 'Blitz' of the provinces.

During that time Huddersfield had nine separate nights of bomb 'incidents'. The first was on 25 August 1940 when ten bombs were dropped on Meltham. The only casualty was a pony cut by flying splinters from a bomb which fell in a field. House windows were broken and slates dislodged, and a water main fractured in Marsden Road. The last was on 12 June 1941 when in the early hours of the morning hundreds of incendiaries and a few high explosives were dropped over a wide area including Almondbury, Lowerhouses, Newsome, Lockwood and Primrose Hill. Civil Defence workers and householders dealt successfully with the incendiaries, although the premises of one or two firms were gutted. At houses in Newsome, one incendiary bomb fell onto a bed and another one into a bath! At Honley there were casualties among the poultry when a bomb fell near a farm.

On 12 December 1940 Batley suffered its worst raid when several homes were destroyed or severely damaged, and hundreds of windows were cracked or broken. A soldier was killed and other people were injured by bomb splinters. Many people were evacuated from their homes due to a number of delayed action bombs. Bombs also fell in Gomersal, Mirfield and Dewsbury. In Savile Town, Dewsbury, a direct hit demolished four houses and killed two women, mother and daughter. A bomb which fell near Wakefield Road wrecked Shaw Cross Colliery offices, killing three employees and injuring another. The raid of 12 December 1940 lasted for a few hours and incendiary bombs 'fell almost like rain in all parts of the district'.

Many local people can recall the nights the *Luftwaffe* attacked their towns and villages. Their reminiscences include some of the many 'near misses' this area was lucky to have escaped with.

"There were one dropped - and it were a big 'un - in Wakefield Cutting at Dewsbury. And it made a hole i' that road, it blew a row of houses down altogether, and [Crawshaw] & Warburtons had a pit at t'other side, all that, and you could have buried a double decker bus in it, in t'crater."
ROBERTTOWN MAN BORN 1912

"I remember one night we were on fire-watch duty and I was in the shop up Northgate [Dewsbury] ... I remember quite clearly one night we were on the top of these buildings when they were coming to bomb Leeds ... the 'planes were so low passing over we could see the pilots in the 'planes, in the enemy 'planes, and that's when they dropped the land mine in Wakefield Road ... and when we got home [we'd] no windows, we were so near, and of course we had to have the windows boarded up."
DEWSBURY WOMAN BORN 1897

AIR RAIDS

"I was dragged by my mother - I was in bed - I was dragged across the street to a shelter at a works ... and we could hear the guns, the guns were making a tremendous noise. There were some anti-aircraft guns in the Dewsbury area, at Caulms Wood I believe, and this was very noisy but I'd more or less slept through it, but my mother woke me up and took me into the shelter. And I remember hearing one bomb - I think it was the high explosive bomb which fell on Mount Pleasant which wasn't very far away really - and this was just the one, and we heard it coming down and this was a most terrifying sound as it came down. It did seem as though it was right overhead and we all thought that we were in for it ... and I remember at the time of the explosion everybody bent over. We were sitting on long bench forms the length of the shelter and everybody sort of bent over and cringed. I was looking down the shelter, and the shelter was made of steel with steel ribs which were bolted together, so you could see going into the distance all these steel ribs. And I remember at the explosion the whole lot, the whole shelter shook, and I could see these steel ribs they actually bounced. And that's the only one, the nearest that I've been - it wasn't really near but it wasn't very pleasant."
BATLEY MAN BORN 1926

"One time coming home from work, and I was at Milnsbridge waiting for a bus down the side of Hirst and Mallinson's Mill and heard the guns going. The searchlights came on and caught a German plane in the lights - the lights were stationed at Almondbury Bank ... they caught the plane in the lights and traced it and the guns started firing. They didn't hit it. I don't know what happened to it, but he must have got away. Nothing crashed round here anyway."
GOLCAR MAN BORN 1922

"... there were a bomb dropped in a field not so far from where I lived and it made a right big crater. In fact some o' t'cows were down t'crater that were in t'field - they just fell down, just went into t'crater. And then there were a soldier killed. He were trying to get out o' t'air raids, and he were running home to get into t'shelter."
LIVERSEDGE WOMAN BORN 1910
AUXILIARY POLICEWOMAN

TWO HORSES KILLED.

When bombs fell near a North East town for the first time early yesterday they killed a horse and bruised another so severely that it had to be destroyed. The animals, both of considerable value, belonged to Mr. Fred Archer, a farmer. Two bombs were dropped in a field from which the hay-crop had recently been gathered.

"There were two bombs dropped at Mirfield in some fields up Wood Lane ... and all that happened there - there were two big craters and they killed two horses."
ROBERTTOWN MAN BORN 1912

"One time when I was working on nights at David Brown's I was working a machine ... I was sat watching the machine running with me back against the wall, when I bounced off the wall into the middle of the floor with this bomb they dropped in Honley Woods, which was about a mile away. And the shock of the bomb made the walls bounce - and me bounce!"
GOLCAR MAN BORN 1922

R 74924
County Borough of Huddersfield

After an Air Raid
?
All the Answers

Issued by
SAMUEL PROCTER,
A.R.P. Controller.

Town Clerk's Office,
Huddersfield.   December, 1940.

The Householder should keep this card with his Identity Card, and see that every member of his household is acquainted with its contents.

The various addresses of premises given are those to which applications should be made for different kinds of assistance—**if the particular premises should be bombed other addresses will be given out by loud speaker vans at the earliest opportunity.**

Look out for the loud speaker vans and listen carefully to the instructions given.

After an Air Raid? All the Answers. This leaflet informed householders of what they should do and where they should go for assistance if their home was damaged or destroyed in an air raid.

"One night my bed shook and it was when they'd dropped one up at Oakes there y'know the mill - is it Pat Martin's Mill? - had got one."
HUDDERSFIELD WOMAN 1915

"... one Christmas time we had to be evacuated because there was an unexploded bomb in Martin's Mill dam, so we were away from home for three or four days, but we had to go on to some relations on Thornhill Road and stay there over the time till it was time to go back, but I don't think it exploded ... we took t'bedding down from our house, and we'd it on the floor because there were four of us with a family, and we took the mattress ... so we'd to sleep on the floor, so that wasn't much of a Christmas was it?"
HUDDERSFIELD WOMAN BORN 1896

"At Salendine Nook, where the school is now, there were some light bombs scattered - I went to look at the craters in the field."
GOLCAR MAN BORN 1922

"One night when the war had been going on for a while he [husband] came running up, and I had an awful bad cold, and I was in bed with this cold and it was about two o'clock in the morning. He says 'Get up!' I says 'I can't get up. I'd rather die in my bed'. So, they struck a house just round the corner in Smiths Avenue [Marsh] ..."
HUDDERSFIELD WOMAN BORN 1899

BY GUM, SHOULDN'T I LOOK DAFT IF WE HAD AN AIR RAID NOW!

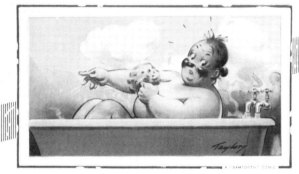

SUNK WITHOUT WARNING, CONSHTABLE.—YOU'D BETTER REPORT IT TO WINSHTON!

"We saw the Sheffield raid, when Sheffield was badly bombed. You could see it all drawing up you know, over those hills over there ... and you could hear like distant thunder all the time you know, and every now and again you could see anti-aircraft shells like little stars straight over them hills there."
MIRFIELD MAN BORN 1922

"From our attic we could see Bradford and Leeds being bombed and the flames, and we could hear the bombs falling."
HUDDERSFIELD WOMAN BORN 1899

"There was a flying bomb raid - the V1. It was one Christmas, my girlfriend, as she was at the time, and myself had been to a dance at Slaithwaite, walked home, seeing her home - she only lived 100 yards from me. Go down home, got into bed and the flying bomb came over and everyone I talked to afterwards was convinced that flying bomb had gone over their roof between their chimneys ... it eventually exploded at Grange Moor but everyone I talked to in Golcar and other areas said it had gone over their house."
GOLCAR MAN BORN 1922

AIR RAIDS

IF HITLER WAS DOWN BELOW US NOW, WOULD I BOMB HIM? **YOU BET I WOULD!**

"At Castle Hill there used to be a large naval gun. Now there was a track over here to Sheffield and places like that for the bombers and they used to go over. Now they always used to say that the man who was in charge of that naval gun had had his wife and family killed in an air raid in somewhere like Plymouth. Consequently whenever these bombers went over he used to open fire and I mean they did open fire regularly and shrapnel used to fall all over! Eventually they moved him and they stopped doing this but shrapnel did use to fall all around here. Now then, one night we were ready for opening the [fish] shop and there was a queue right up to this corner, there was always a queue before you opened y'know, and this gun opened up and me dad says 'Oh bloody 'ell' he says 'that's it, we've 'ad it now, they'll all go'. And when he opened the door not a soul had moved - they were still in the queue. There was shrapnel falling, and the only concession that had been made to that shrapnel was the man in the end house went in and fetched his umbrella, and he stood there with his umbrella up. Well we laughed when we saw - he stood there with his umbrella as though its going to stop these huge pieces of shrapnel that were falling!"
HUDDERSFIELD WOMAN BORN 1925

"They dropped a big bomb in the river across from our house, at the bridge, by Colne Road bridge - but it was a huge bomb and they put it in the market place ... oh, it seemed enormous to me you know because I wasn't that old then, but it was a great big thing and there was writing all over it in German you know."
HUDDERSFIELD WOMAN BORN 1931

"... up Gomersal there were some searchlights on the barley fields up by Popeley Farm and these operated in conjunction with some anti-aircraft guns which were situated at Caulms Wood at Dewsbury, and there was the Observer Corps post on the barley field which is still there today. And they apparently tried to bomb the searchlights this particular night and they dropped, I think there were three bombs - one probably about a hundred to fifty yards off the searchlights, one just at the other side of the houses on Oxford Road and one in the cricket field. And the one on the cricket field it was thought hadn't detonated, and we were all evacuated to a house which is below the California Mills, what were the California Mills, at Gomersal and we'd to spend a night there ... and they discovered eventually that it was a dud bomb was that particular one."
GOMERSAL MAN BORN 1928

"... the anti-aircraft guns sited locally were popping away and one of the things that we seemed to have to watch was the falling shrapnel from the shells that were exploding up there, rather than enemy action. So we didn't see a lot of enemy action. There was just a couple of nights when I was at Brook's when bombs were dropped fairly close, you know, we had a crunch fairly close. I remember one, I think it was somewhere round Kings Mill Lane, by the bridge at the bottom of Newsome Road, and there was a company there that had a hit and that was a crunchy one that night."
NEW MILL MAN BORN 1920
FIRE-WATCHER, BROOK MOTOR'S

ALL COUNTRIES HAVE THEIR BOMB-PROOF SHELTERS, **POLAND** INCLUDED!

"George Hudson had [a furniture warehouse] up Station Road at Batley ... and Station Road had been roped off because of an unexploded bomb. Now at the time Mr Hudson hadn't a delivery van of his own. He used a general delivery man ... And we needed some furniture out. I went with him and when we got to the entrance of Station Road there was a rope across 'NO ENTRY - UNEXPLODED BOMB', and - incredible - we went through this! We lifted this, and we went through it, and we loaded up the furniture and went out again - of all the stupid things! I mean, in retrospect, absolutely stupid! I mean I was only a boy, but the man, he was a man and I suppose he should have known better."
BATLEY MAN BORN 1926

"... there was one evening, week time evening, when there were some bombs dropped on Batley, and there were anti-aircraft guns all around, were fighting like billy-o. And we silly young beggars were out in the road outside the drill hall - not wearing steel helmets, wearing forage caps - and listening to the shrapnel falling. Can you believe - I mean, you know, it only needed one piece of shrapnel to hit someone right on top of the head and that was 'Goodbye'!"
HIGHTOWN MAN BORN 1920
HOME GUARD

"We used to sit outside and watch them coming over and they even used to wave to us did the pilots, they came so low y'know. And one old lady that lived by us - I'd been washing and it was a lovely night, and I'd all me washing out and she came down, she says 'Jerry's coming, Jerry's coming'. I says 'Well, what about it?' She says 'Well fetch that washing in, he'll be able to see where we are'. I says 'Oh well never mind him, I'm not fetching my washing in for Jerry.'"
HUDDERSFIELD WOMAN BORN 1902

NORTH EAST "BLITZ"

Hundreds of Incendiary Bombs
Soldier Killed

Nazi 'planes visited a North-East town last night in the course of their attacks and caused a few fires.

A number of people had to evacuate their homes pending the disposal of unexploded bombs.

A soldier was killed by shrapnel.

The fires were handled with great skill by the A.F.S., who received much assistance from soldiers.

The attack began in the early evening with baskets of incendiary bombs, some of which set alight buildings not far from the town centre.

The fire bombs did little damage to house property and one housewife caught a bomb in a bucket of water as it tore through her ceiling!

The incendiary bombs were handled with remarkable speed by the air raid wardens and members of the public and were quickly smothered with sand. Stirrup pumps also prevented many serious fires.

Mr. A. Shillito tackled two incendiaries which fell between large buildings but more landed nearby and set sheds alight. The A.F.S. trailer pumps soon put out the blaze in a smaller shed, but the larger was burnt out.

Mr. Norman Wilson found a fire bomb in his garage and soldiers extinguished it.

Fire in another large building menaced the local first-aid depot, but the volunteers, at great risk, removed to safety the motor ambulance waggons and most of the first-aid stores.

While this fire was burning Mr. James F. Ineson dashed through the flames with a fireman and retrieved from the safe in his firm's office a number of valuable documents.

Throughout the operations in this area Superintendent Horace Horne and members of the first-aid parties worked like Trojans. The handiness of buckets of water, sand and stirrup pumps undoubtedly saved the St. John Ambulance headquarters and a storage building opposite.

Mr. Horne was taking a class of ambulance cadets when the first bombs fell and the young people assisted in the operations.

Sergeants Whittle and Fletcher, Corporal Tracy and Driver Stephenson, with another comrade, saved a laundry by fighting the flames from the roof of a nearby building. These soldiers also checked an outbreak in a mineral water works.

This action was particularly heroic in view of the fact that the soldiers knew that an unexploded high explosive bomb was not far away.

Furniture had to be carried from two houses which it was impossible to save from fire.

Four unexploded bombs were soon traced and over 100 people had to take temporary refuge in local schools.

A cinema was hit by an incendiary bomb, but little damage was done. Other bombs fell in fields and some shop windows were broken.

In an adjoining town some houses were demolished and a woman and her daughter were dead when rescued.

BOMBS AWAY FROM HOME

Although serious bomb incidents were few in Kirklees, many local people faced danger in other parts of the country. Men and women in the Forces, essential war work, or Fire and Rescue Services sent to blitzed cities, experienced many of the traumas and dangers faced by the residents of those cities. Here a Wren from Huddersfield, based in London during the war, relates some of her experiences.

"The V1 [Doodlebug] started coming over about June or July [1944] and they were frightening because you could hear them coming along like an ordinary small aeroplane now, and then suddenly it stopped, the engine cut off, and you knew it was going to drop. And then suddenly 'Oh no!' - a mighty explosion and it had landed somewhere you see. And you thought, 'Oh thank God it hasn't landed on me'. But if you were very close to it you could hear it whistling down. It was frightening. And we had to take all our bunks and bedding and sleep down in the cellars at Quarters ... it wasn't very nice and there were cockroaches running about on the floor. We hated it.

IN BLITZED AREAS

Batley A.F.S. Men Under Fire

RESCUE PARTIES ON HUMBERSIDE

It can now be revealed that in the recent heavy air attacks on Merseyside and Humberside, Batley's Auxiliary Fire Service and Rescue and Demolition Parties gave valuable assistance to the harassed Civil Defence services of those localities.

The firemen distinguished themselves and in both areas earned the respect of the men of the units with whom they were associated.

One of the men recently returned from Lancashire told a *News* reporter, "In spite of the conditions prevailing at the time, the people in the bombed towns were wonderful and would do anything for the firemen. Some of them even went out of their way to shake hands with us."

"One of the girls lived in east London, and her mother said, 'Oh well bring some of them for the weekend', you know, 'have a good nights sleep here'. ... Her mother played the piano and we all had a good singsong, and we were singing 'Pedro the Fisherman' oh, very heartily and loudly when suddenly there was a great explosion. And because we were singing we hadn't heard the Doodlebug coming you see. All the lights went out, plaster started dropping from the ceiling and the glass from the windows all came in and we were all choking with dust and soot. Course it was dark, it was black dark ... we had to pick our way through the house and out into the back garden where they had a shelter sort of half submerged in the garden, and spent the rest of the night in there ... the bomb had actually fallen in the next street where two or three houses had been demolished ... people were killed.

"We heard another coming over during the morning ... it had cut out but you could hear it whistling, and we knew it was coming somewhere very near. In fact it fell on the chapel in Wellington Barracks. It was full of people at a service and many were killed and the place was demolished. It was a real tragedy. Some of our Wrens were there, was full of service people and their friends. And that's the next building to ours, and of course when it landed there was this terrific explosion and, well I was just swept off my feet ... and into the next room ...

"... all the trees were stripped of leaves - they were in full green leaf all the way down and they were just stripped off and all laid on the road with the force of the explosion. And of course the fire engine and ambulances were all coming to rescue these people who were in Wellington Barracks. It was terrible. So we got on the train and we went up onto Hampstead Heath actually, and we all just laid there on the Heath and we all just cried. And after that, well that frightened us, we didn't go out very much after that. We stopped going to the theatre because we just felt you know we couldn't take the risk."

HUDDERSFIELD WOMAN BORN 1923
WREN

INCENDIARIES

The main hazard for local people during air raids were incendiary bombs specifically designed to set property on fire and dropped hundreds at a time. Some German bombers could carry up to 2,000 incendiaries. These bombs had intentionally poor ballistic properties and spread out as they fell, thus increasing the chances of starting a number of fires. The bombs could be dealt with using sand, or water and a stirrup pump, provided immediate and correct action was taken. Much information was distributed by the Ministry of Home Security to instruct and encourage the general public as well as Civil Defence workers to tackle the bombs immediately.

Practising with a stirrup pump. Stirrup pumps were used for extinguishing newly ignited incendiary bombs, as well as for dealing with fires caused by them.

"I said 'It's been murder up Lowerhouses with the incendiary bombs and what not, and the guns firing away and planes coming over'. Anyway I said 'Haven't you heard anything?' She said 'No', so I said 'Well you've got an incendiary bomb through your attic!' Now their house it had been one house and it had been made into two houses but the attic went over the whole lot, but it had gone through the back half. Now the people in the back half, t'Wardens had been trying to knock them up but couldn't make head nor tail out of them. And there'd also been another bomb dropped on Kings Mill Lane and so I said, 'You are a lot aren't you, sleeping through all that'. Well she hadn't heard a thing!"
HUDDERSFIELD WOMAN BORN 1902

"... one of them [incendiaries] dropped through the roof of George Hudson's furniture shop. I remember the following morning when we went into work the terrible smell of fire which had been damped down by the National Fire Service people. They'd flooded the place. Everything was saturated with water and in the basement there was about two or three feet of water. I remember George Hudson sending us to the shop but one next door to get some wellingtons to go down there, and we were trying to salvage what we could and it was utter chaos ... Half way through the day there was a panic on because someone smelt burning and in fact up in the roof space the thing had started smouldering again, and so the NFS were sent for and a man appeared with a stirrup pump ... Two people were a team for this ... and guess who went up in the roof space? I went up and we damped things down again and I remember doing this!"
BATLEY MAN BORN 1926

"We got loads [of incendiaries] up Fanny Moor Lane. They was all dropping down the street, they kept dropping down and people were going out - we'd got the sand and the shovels and that - and putting them out. It was women that was coming out in their night-dresses and putting them out, because most of the men was away y'see!"
HUDDERSFIELD WOMAN BORN 1902

"Ooh and there were incendiaries going all up and down Old Bank but luckily everything escaped. And then t'next farm to Pogg Farm, Bullace Tree Farm - he dropped another load on there, and it were just after harvest time but nowt got afire there."
ROBERTTOWN MAN BORN 1912
THRESHER

INCENDIARIES

In 1941 the Government introduced compulsory fire-watching for men and women. Streets, schools, commercial and industrial premises and other public buildings had fire-watchers patrolling every night, normally drawn from their own residents or workforce. Although the Fire Service did not have a massive task in the Kirklees area, many local firemen were sent to severely bombed areas such as Kent, Manchester and Sheffield where they faced great dangers.

"My father had to go and fire-watch at his work and the teachers at school did as well. They had to sleep at school in turn, so many each night on camp beds and what not to make sure the place wasn't set on fire with incendiary bombs."
KIRKHEATON WOMAN BORN 1921

"I was in digs and I was with two very old people, neither of them well and everyone was supposed to do a night of fire-watching so I did their nights as well as my own. And the night that Bradford was bombed, the shrapnel was coming down in chunks, and the next morning the door and the garden had lumps of shrapnel in it from the bombing, and you now and then heard the 'Ping' as something hit your helmet that night. That happened to be one of the nights I was on duty!"
HIGHTOWN WOMAN BORN 1919

"Everyone who worked was called upon to spend one evening, at least one evening per week, in patrolling their place of work to watch out for fires and to put out, hopefully to put out, fires which had been started by fire-bombs. So one had to spend a full evening. Most people would play cards and eventually would sleep a little in a small bed, a small truckle type bed with rather dirty evil smelling blankets which always used to put me off, but eventually nature used to overcome and I used to fall asleep ... Some of the older men who didn't wish to spend a night out of their own comfortable bed would bribe us youngsters there in offering us their three and sixpence or three shillings or whatever it was to take over their duty, and as we were always short of money we used to quite often fire-watch two or even three nights a week depending on the state of our finances at the time!"
BATLEY MAN BORN 1926

A Kilo-Magnesium Incendiary Bomb.

"... we had a fire thing at Brook's [Brook Motors], fire-watchers, you know, and they used to go on the roof. If the alarm sounded everybody else went down into the dug-out cellars, and those that had been recruited for this air raid patrol, air raid warden stuff, they went on the roof, you know, to watch anything that was happening. And the things would come over, the aeroplanes, and occasionally we had incidents where incendiaries were dropped - we didn't have anything dropped on our factory."
NEW MILL MAN BORN 1920

IN THE SHELTERS

When the siren sounded, most people took shelter from possible air attack. Many houses in Kirklees had cellars which could be used as air raid shelters. For those without cellars there were communal air raid shelters, or Government issue Anderson shelters for outside some individual homes. By May 1940 Dewsbury had provided shelter for 8,000 persons in public surface shelters, tunnels and trenches. Anderson shelters were issued free to those with an income of less than £250 a year. Other people could purchase them if they wished. Around two and a quarter million were issued nationwide, though not everyone erected or used them. One enterprising Birstall farmer built an air raid shelter 'on the Anderson principle' to hold eight cows and a bull, the most valuable cattle of his herd of over thirty, and precious because they were the last in their line of descent.

"We thought - I think this was a feeling amongst a lot of people - that if you were in one of the old houses with the cellar head you were safer there than in many of the air raid shelters."
GOMERSAL MAN BORN 1928

"The Anderson shelter would be fairly good protection against rubble falling but obviously if there was a direct hit on the shelter your number was certainly up!"
HUDDERSFIELD MAN BORN 1927

Anderson shelters were cold, dark and gloomy and because they were partially sunk below ground level - wet! People tried to make them more comfortable and homely but there were always problems.

I can remember there was wood, like wood slats across the floor, but underneath the slats there was water. I always remember the water underneath. It was fairly common in air raid shelters - nearly always had water in the base of it."
GOMERSAL MAN BORN 1928

"My first fear of going down into the shelter ... was mice and things y'know - being in your own garden underground. I'm not frightened of creepy crawlies and I'm used to animals on the farm, but I said to my mum 'Have you shaken everything?', y'know before we went to bed we used to shake everything ..."
BIRSTALL WOMAN BORN 1917

The Anderson shelter was made of galvanised corrugated steel sheets, bolted together to provide a shelter 6 feet 6 inches long, 4 feet 6 inches wide and 6 feet high. It was recommended that a hole 3-4 feet deep should be dug in the garden into which to sink the shelter, and that the roof should then be covered with a minimum of 15 inches of soil.

"There was nothing in of course - it was left to the individual to make it as comfortable as possible, so most people put in chicken wire type bunk beds and so forth. They were always very damp, bedding was damp. Most people 'd take their bedding out and bring it in. If the sirens went then people would emerge from the house there with an armful of bedding, thermos flasks, with first aid equipment and so forth, with books and candles ..."
BATLEY MAN BORN 1926

"... she [mother] used to do lace work ... and even on the inside [of the shelter] she hung a curtain and put lace at the bottom to try and make it home from home ... I think she could make a wooden box home could my mum you know, with her little ideas."
BIRSTALL WOMAN BORN 1917

IN THE SHELTERS

WHEN THE AIR RAID WARNINGS SHRIEK OUT LOUD
WHAT FUNNY SIGHTS THERE'LL BE,
PEOPLE DASHING OUT DISTRESSED,
SOME IN NIGHTIES, SOME UNDRESSED!
OH, DAMN THE BLACK-OUT---IT'S TOO DARK TO SEE!

Memories of hurrying to the shelters as the siren sounded, and of what it felt like to be inside as enemy planes flew overhead, are strong amongst local people.

"When we went to bed every night we had to put them [clothes] in a pile ready for getting on - you know, your vest on the top and sort of screwed up ready to pull over your head. I used to do the same for my sister. And for years and years and years after I used to do it - I couldn't break myself of the habit. And even now that feeling comes back to me when I'm getting dressed. It was a mixture of everything - the panic, you know, and the feeling you've got to get them on quick. And sometimes my mum used to just pick us up with clothes and everything and get us in the shelter and then dress us."
CLECKHEATON WOMAN BORN 1932

"We used to sing and I could play the accordion, piano-accordion, an' I'd take me accordion across if we'd time. Or if it went on a long time somebody'd say to me dad 'Go fetch your accordion' and we'd play and we'd all sing, and t'more noise we made t'less we could hear the aeroplanes and we'd get carried away singing and that was it."
HECKMONDWIKE WOMAN BORN 1926

"Well, it were an atmosphere of fear. Everybody thought it could be their turn next you know. Nearly everybody talked about 'Oh it's getting nearer', or 'that's not so far away' you know, as though they were wondering what it's going to be t'next time. They all had that same fear."
LIVERSEDGE WOMAN BORN 1910
ARP WARDEN

Not everyone took advantage of air raid shelters in this area, particularly as the war progressed.

"Early on you used to get up every time and go down, early on in the war, but then when sort of nothing much happened you didn't bother ... You'd perhaps get up and sit in your room and be comfy and make a cup of tea or something but not go down in the cellar."
HUDDERSFIELD WOMAN BORN 1915

"Oh, everybody knew what to do, but we didn't go into the shelter and my children wouldn't go in either. They seemed to want to be there and see what's going on - except the one who wanted to stay in bed. But yes, we were all right because we were there in the road - everybody listening and watching, and if anything had happened you're on the spot. Much better than being in a shelter."
HUDDERSFIELD WOMAN BORN 1896

"Well the siren [All Clear] used to go. Everybody heard it and of course they were like rabbits. Everybody came out o' their hiding holes then, out o' cellars and shelters and wherever they'd been. It were busy - everybody came out and brought their jewellery and their wills and what have you back with 'em and started again."
LIVERSEDGE WOMAN BORN 1910
ARP WARDEN

ALWAYS CARRY YOUR GAS MASK

As poisonous gases had been used in the First World War it was at first anticipated that they would be used again. Everyone in the country was issued with a Respirator or 'gas mask', varying in type according to the persons age and size, to protect them against breathing any of the known war gases. Leaflets were also issued giving instructions to civilians on how to cope with gas attacks. Though everyone at first acknowledged the necessity for gas masks, they did not enjoy carrying them everywhere, or practising putting them on. Even the gas mask carrying cases were subject to fashion ideas.

"... dad weren't a young man, he were forty-odd and he'd been in the First World War and ... my dad had chronic bronchitis, and he died of that, and he always said it were with having this mustard gas during the First World War. So my dad thought it were great to get these, you know - make sure they get them and they fit 'em properly. So we were taught through my dad that we must have these gas masks and we should put them on at all times ... a lot of men of my dad's age were bronchial so we knew that it were a good thing really to have this gas mask and we sort of had it drummed into us - 'You get one and you wear it' and we had to take it at all times ... so we'd set off and leave it with somebody, you know, somebody that had a young dad that wasn't as keen as mine."
HECKMONDWIKE WOMAN BORN 1926

"... terrible things they were, terrible. You slipped them under your chin, over your head, tightened the straps and - well - Tasmanian Devil couldn't have looked any worse. Just this big thing in front of you - I found it very hard, very difficult to breathe in."
HUDDERSFIELD WOMAN BORN 1924

"They weren't comfortable at all. The plastic, kind of plastic eyepiece steamed up when you were breathing - you couldn't really see in them ... from the comfort point of view they were a washout."
GOLCAR MAN BORN 1922

"... they were horrible, you could taste the rubber in them, they were awful. And t'kids used to scream when you put 'em on. We'd a niece ... we used to nearly hold her down, you know. At t'finish, when she'd got fitted, we didn't put it on her again. They used to say ' Keep trying to get them used to it', but they go hysterical - she just didn't like it. So once she got it on, we knew she were fitted up, so that was it. We took it with us but we never put it on her because she used to fight it, you know, scream and carry on."
HECKMONDWIKE WOMAN BORN 1926

"... a lot of people were frightened of 'em. They were frightened of putting 'em on and - 'If I have to die, I have to die, that's all'. They wouldn't be bothered. You had to persuade 'em to wear it, and make sure they did wear it, and for their own good. But of course there again you can't be with 'em all the time."
LIVERSEDGE WOMAN BORN 1910
ARP WARDEN

GOOD THING COWS DON'T FLY, OR WE SHOULD NEED GAS MASKS!

NEWS CH
AIR DEFENCE SCHEME

"... they were in a cardboard box, and string on and hung over their shoulder ... Well of course the fashion became then that you made covers for your gas mask and some made leather ones or material, velvet, some to match their outfits. It used to be a fashion and I was very disgusted because the service respirators didn't have a fancy cover."
HIGHTOWN WOMAN BORN 1919
FIRST AID WARDEN

ALWAYS CARRY YOUR GAS MASK

Babies were given a 'Protective Helmet' which caused much consternation amongst mothers, as the often reluctant baby had to be placed almost totally inside. The operation of the helmet depended on someone pumping air into it at a rate of 35 - 45 pumps per minute. The fact that pumping could be stopped for several minutes if necessary could not have offered much reassurance to worried mothers. Government instructions were issued, and classes were held locally to train in their use. Many local people however do not seem to have been totally confident in their effectiveness.

"We had one of the big ones for the baby but I never got him into it. I don't know what'd have happened if - he used to scream heavens high. I used to think 'Well I'll have to get him used to this darned thing', but I never really got him into it, I never got him really fastened up in it ... They were horrible, I mean, y'know they were frightening for a child to be put in, but I suppose if there'd have been gas and things you'd have just rammed him in and he'd have had to yell wouldn't he? But practising was a nightmare."
HUDDERSFIELD WOMAN BORN 1915

The red 'Mickey Mouse' young child's gas masks, for children of between approximately two and five years old, were much more acceptable, especially when children discovered the rude noises they could make by blowing out of them!

"The kids had been issued with gas masks, y'know the Mickey Mouse gas masks. Well, all the kids wanted their gas masks on and they was all going round 'grunt, grunt, grunt' like little pigs crunching away. You couldn't tell a word they was saying! And they wouldn't take them off - the novelty did wear off after a while but the kids thought it was grand."
HUDDERSFIELD WOMAN BORN 1902

ARP Wardens and other Civil Defence personnel were issued with service respirators. As part of their training they had to experience wearing them in gas.

"We had to all wear gas masks and be put through this chamber to see how you reacted to it ... it were like a big artic[ulated] lorry ... and you used to have to walk through this and stop a bit and breath a bit an' just lift your gas mask off to see what it smelt like and how you felt - give you a chance of knowing what you were looking for, and you had to put it on again."
LIVERSEDGE WOMAN BORN 1910
ARP WARDEN

Young child's 'Mickey Mouse' gas mask. These were designed to look like toys in an attempt to take the fear out of wearing gas masks.

No 2 Anti-gas ointment for the treatment of skin affected by liquid blister gas.

As the war years progressed and gas was not used people began to relax their attitude towards always carrying their gas mask.

CIVIL DEFENCE WORKERS

Every neighbourhood had a network of Civil Defence personnel to take action before, during, and after air raids. Fire Service, ARP, rescue, ambulance, police, first aid and WVS personnel were on alert each night, ready to mobilise instantly if required. They were often at risk, working outside during air raids instead of being in the safety of the shelters. Hundreds of local men and women undertook these duties, many voluntarily, some giving up their few free hours away from work to be there in case of emergency. Kirklees Civil Defence workers were not confined to the Kirklees area only, and in particular, local rescue and fire fighting personnel undertook dangerous duties in other parts of the country. Local people have revealed something of their day to day life as part of these services.

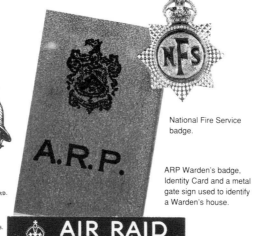

National Fire Service badge.

ARP Warden's badge, Identity Card and a metal gate sign used to identify a Warden's house.

"We were there [on duty] until two and three and four o'clock in the morning and then we'd go to work. Yes we'd to come home, have a meal and have a bath and go to work."
DEWSBURY WOMAN BORN 1897
ARP WARDEN

"... if you were called out or t'buzzer went - the sirens - you had to go out whether you'd been on duty or you were due to go on duty, or even if you were in bed you had to get up and go down to t'ARP house. You all had to congregate there and then you were all sent in different directions ... we were always on call, whatever time of day or night it was, we were always on call."
LIVERSEDGE WOMAN BORN 1910
ARP WARDEN

A Civil Defence Rally advertisement. Such rallies and competitions were a part of training procedures and also a form of public entertainment. At a Spen Valley ARP area competition for mobile units and first-aid parties, held in September 1941, the competing teams were Mirfield, Batley, Heckmondwike and Spenborough. Tests included an imitation bomb incident which caused the demolition of mills, and casualties. Batley's team came first, and went on to compete in the semi-finals of a County competition.

"I worked twelve hours a day but it wasn't really hard work, that was very, very easy. I taught first aiders. I taught St. John's Ambulance people the little bit more than they learned in St. John's Ambulance - how to give injections and that sort of thing, and we prepared dressings and everything ... We had definite arrangements made whereby if there was a raid what would happen, and we also had practice raids ... We'd get the red warning by telephone, that meant there was an air raid, then you'd hear the sirens go ... We had the incendiaries that came over Cleckheaton, right across, right along the railway station, and the incendiaries dropped into houses, and the ARP people were out and everyone was out, and we had one or two burns that night to deal with."
HIGHTOWN WOMAN BORN 1919
FIRST AID WARDEN

"... you could be sent anywhere, like once we had to go out for a doctor at Batley - we'd a big bomb in Batley - and we went for this doctor. He had to be at t'ARP house and we went to fetch him. Well, we went down a crater. You couldn't see where you were going 'cause there's no lights!"
LIVERSEDGE WOMAN BORN 1910
AUXILIARY POLICEWOMAN

"If it'd been reported that somebody had some coupons that they were spending rather lavishly you wanted to find out where they were getting 'em from. You went for deserters that'd absconded from the Army, Navy or Air Force and bringing them into the Headquarters ... You had rather a busy life, but interesting ... Now we once had a woman that got a lot of clothes and we couldn't understand where she got all her coupons from.
Anyway, she'd been pinching 'em evidently, and she finished up i' Strangeways, we took her to Strangeways Jail. And they wanted her every time she did owt like that because she were a right good ironer, and they wanted her in to do t'ironing!"
LIVERSEDGE WOMAN BORN 1910
AUXILIARY POLICEWOMAN

LOOK AT THAT, YOU FOOL---AND YOU MADE AN AIR RAID WARDEN THIS MORNING!

A "BAMFORTH" COMIC

ABSENT-MINDED WARDEN: "WHERE DID I PUT THAT BLINKING HELMET LAST NIGHT?"

A "BAMFORTH" COMIC

"There was no class distinction, there were people amongst our ARP, rich and poor alike, you all fitted in together into the work that was to be done and you got on so well together ... We had this lady who was pretty wealthy, and another one whose father was the leading architect, and we had someone who owned quite a few shoe shops. There used to be three of us on duty every night, sleeping duty, and they would take their tops off and sleep in their pants and slips and they'd have the most expensive underwear on, some had probably come from America or somewhere like that, and we'd be very ordinary, but there would be nobody say anything about that. And there was no one bringing anything in that was better than anyone else. No, no class distinction whatsoever, you were all alike in the war."
HIGHTOWN WOMAN BORN 1919
ARP WARDEN

"... we were down in the cellars of the ARP headquarters. We all went down, down in Cleckheaton - there were an old mill, corn mill, and we went down there. And you used to have a bucket behind the curtain one end. And it had a seat, a long seat and a bit of heating on and plenty of coffee, plenty of tea going and things like that, box of biscuits, and you sat and you sang and talked together. And then someone would say 'I'll have to go behind the curtain now'. This was men and women, and so we all start whistling, and all start singing, and as I say we made a joke of it all. We didn't take it seriously and then of course when the 'All Clear' went we all came up."
HIGHTOWN WOMAN BORN 1919
ARP WARDEN

"One night we had a yellow warning, so this was gas, and two of us put our gas masks ready and set off up the road where we were told this gas had fallen - gas bombs. Went up the road and finally we came to a field where they'd been spreading muck! So we came back and we gave them the 'All Clear'."
HIGHTOWN WOMAN BORN 1919
ARP WARDEN

KITCHEN FRONT

Food rationing was introduced in January 1940, beginning with sugar, butter, ham and bacon, followed by a whole range of foodstuffs including meat, tea, cheese, fats, conserves and eggs. As escalating merchant shipping casualties led to greater food shortages in late 1940, 1941 and 1942, an increasing number of food items had their distribution controlled. Examples of ration allowances per person per week in 1941 were 1 ounce of cheese, 2 ounces tea, 4 ounces bacon or ham, 8 ounces fats, 8 ounces sugar and 1s. 2d. worth of meat. Every person in the country had a precious ration book without which they could not legally buy the rationed goods.

Local people welcomed rationing which aimed to ensure that the limited foodstuffs were distributed fairly and equally. Careful management of rations was important to prevent being left without at the end of the week. Swapping of ration coupons was common when people did not like or could not afford certain foodstuffs on ration. Even though people had the coupons, they did not necessarily have enough money to buy the rationed goods.

"... you'd only those little portions, but you did get those portions because you were on ration which was a good thing. You all got the same and you'd always a little bit."
HUDDERSFIELD WOMAN BORN 1896

"You used to go to the shop for your two ounces of this and your quarter of that, and the grocer had a pair of scissors there behind the counter - he used to cut the coupon off. You could not go again till you were due to go again - you couldn't get anything over the ration."
GOLCAR MAN BORN 1922

"You'd to be practical. Y'see some people - I mean I knew people - they just went mad. Y'see when they got their rations they'd have a big baking day and then eat it all up! Well, they'd nothing then y'see. You'd to be very frugal and make it spin out."
HUDDERSFIELD WOMAN BORN 1915

"... when the coupons were done for that week, you see they took 'em out weekly, you couldn't go and get a month's supply straight away ... and of course when it were done it were done. And therefore you had to scrounge off your neighbours then - and if you couldn't, or they hadn't it, well, you had to do without and that was all there was to it."
LIVERSEDGE WOMAN BORN 1910

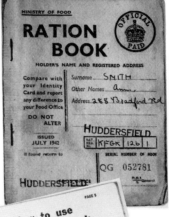

General Ration Books, 1942.

"... you did it quite legitimately. There would be a lady who would have six children and she said 'Oh I can't afford all my sugar, I can't afford all my butter ration, I can't afford my margarine, but if somebody'll exchange me something of theirs'. So we weren't keen on bacon, so I'd say 'Have my bacon ration and I'll have your sugar and butter ration' and we did it that way."
HIGHTOWN WOMAN BORN 1919

"All I could afford to get were three pennyworth of stewing beef and I used to make a dinner out of it - it was very poor times ... they were nearly all alike, all t'soldiers wives."
HUDDERSFIELD WOMAN BORN 1916.

KITCHEN FRONT

Local people coped well with rationing, finding ways to make the most of restricted food supplies, though many recall how much effort was required to feed the family. Large families fared better than those living alone as rations could be pooled, but friends and neighbours also combined their allowances. Although diets lacked variety, those who could afford to buy their rations say they never went hungry. Special dietary requirements caused problems, however allowances were usually made.

"... you got two ounce of corned beef per person in your ration - there were just the two of us, four ounce of corned beef. So my neighbour used to say 'If I give you our rations and some potatoes' - he was a farm labourer, the man - 'and some onions, will you make a pasty?' So I used to make an enormous pasty with four ounce of corned beef, more potatoes and onion than corned beef, and we made a good dinner of it."
HIGHTOWN WOMAN BORN 1919

"Another day we'd have some scraps of bacon, not a quarter of a pound, and we'd slice potatoes up and onions again - they were a good stand by - and carrots, and bits of bacon in between. Put that in your oven and that was what we called 'Panaculty'. You'd make a big tin full of that and it filled you. You could go working twelve hours then on that. We were never seriously affected healthwise. We never went short of food."
HIGHTOWN WOMAN BORN 1919

" I can't say that we were hungry. I think we'd a balanced diet you know ... fish and chips thankfully weren't on the ration!"
HUDDERSFIELD WOMAN BORN 1924

"So long as the kids got what they wanted nothing worried me. It didn't worry me what I got and my husband didn't worry - he'd give everything up for the kids."
HUDDERSFIELD WOMAN
BORN 1902

IT'S ALL BECAUSE OF HITLER
YOUR SUGAR RATION'S LITTLER!
IT'S ALL BECAUSE OF HITLER
THE COST OF MILD AND BITTER!
IT'S ALL BECAUSE OF HITLER
THE PETROL RATION'S HIT YER!

BUT REMEMBER THIS, MY FRIEND,
WHEN AT NIGHT YOU
GROPE ABOUT,
ADOLF'S GOING TO PAY FOR THIS---
**HIS LIGHT WILL BE
PUT OUT!**
— D. TEMPEST

"Me eldest son, he was short of sugar. Well, I mean, it was impossible - we only got two ounces of sugar a week per person. Well that doesn't go very far for cooking and things. But he used to have my sugar, his dad's sugar, his grandma's sugar, his grandad's sugar - all our sugar and all our sweets, boiled sweets ... [the] doctor, he says 'He wants sugar!', 'Well' I says 'I can't get him any'. He says 'Well I'll give you this doctors note and you can get glucose and lucozade for him', but I couldn't get it without the doctors note."
HUDDERSFIELD WOMAN BORN 1902

"I was fortunate I suppose - fortunate in one way. I was very, very anaemic after I had my eldest son and I had a note from the doctor to get a ration of liver, which wasn't on ration but it was scarce, so you had to have a note. And I had liver once a week, so I made a meal for all of us with that too."
HIGHTOWN WOMAN BORN 1919

KITCHEN FRONT

Clearly remembered are the long queues which formed for some rationed foods, and particularly for special deliveries of unrationed foods. This was an opportunity to supplement the diet which many people would not miss, even though it often meant hours of waiting. It usually fell to the housewife to spend much of her time queueing for the necessities of life for her family. News of the arrival of goods in the shops quickly spread on the local grapevine!

"If you saw a queue you joined it - it didn't matter what was at the end of it, you just joined it!"
HUDDERSFIELD WOMAN BORN 1927

"... you could go around and if somebody said 'Oranges' you were off like a shot to get your orange per person!"
HIGHTOWN WOMAN BORN 1919

"When anything was coming in and somebody whispered 'There's meat today' naturally everybody was there at the butchers before the poor bloke had opened and cut the darned thing."
BIRSTALL WOMAN BORN 1917

"There was always queues, wherever you went there was queues. Like if a shop got a supply of biscuits in it went all up the streets - everbody knew so everybody queued. But expectant mothers had a special ration book and they could go to the front of the queue - now that's a thing I remember because my mum was expecting."
HUDDERSFIELD WOMAN BORN 1924

"Even onions sometimes I had to queue for because there weren't very many. I always remember once at a whist drive in Slaithwaite the first prize was a large onion, and whoever received it was very pleased to get it!"
HUDDERSFIELD WOMAN BORN 1923

JOE! ASK HIM TO BRING A COUPLE OF BANANAS OUT O' THE BLINKIN' HAT,— THAT'LL FLOOR HIM!

A "BAMFORTH" COMIC

"You couldn't get fruit hardly. I mean you could get an orange now and again, but like bananas and things like that, well, you never saw them. There wasn't any at all. I might get one orange a week and you used to share it."
HUDDERSFIELD WOMAN BORN 1902

"I've queued at the greengrocers at Marsh for fruit, at the Co-op greengrocers where I always shopped. But y'see, there'd be a queue higher up Marsh - well ... I hadn't t'face to go and queue for things that were in short supply when I wasn't a regular customer there! ... These women used to set off in the morning and go round town joining every queue there was - they'd come home y'know, weighed down with all these things that were short."
HUDDERSFIELD WOMAN BORN 1915

"There was a little shop across from David Brown's called Heeley's, I believe that's still there, and we used to get bread there. But Saturday mornings every so often they used to get those buns, it's a bit like tea cake with icing on top, and they weren't nice - French buns they are I believe - and you used to see this queue all t'way round. Anybody would think they'd cream cakes or something but they hadn't, it was these French buns we used to queue for."
HUDDERSFIELD WOMAN BORN 1922

"I remember my sister coming one day and she says 'There's a man coming onto the station and he's bringing crates of rabbits, but he's not coming to any shop, you've to go round to the station to get one'. And my sister got up at six o'clock one morning and went down to the station to get a rabbit. And she came back and she went down to the corner to my other sister that lived near to tell her that she'd got a rabbit ... and when she came back she met the cat down the path with the rabbit. The cat had been in the house and got the rabbit that she'd queued from six o'clock in the morning for!"
DEWSBURY WOMAN BORN 1897

Housewives were urged by the Ministry of Food to help win the war on the 'Kitchen Front'. Wartime cookery books, leaflets, the radio and newspapers all gave tips on how to make the most of that which was available, and how to use substitutes for what was not. Classes and demonstrations of wartime cookery took place all around Kirklees at Technical Colleges and Gas and Electric Showrooms. Recipes appeared for dishes such as Scones without fat, Carrot and Apricot Pie, Potato Scones and Beetroot Mould. Local people took up almost forgotten practices of preserving food, usually home grown, to enrich the winter diet, and made clever improvisations to stretch their rations. Often livestock such as rabbits and chickens were kept to supplement the diet. Some people joined together in Pig Clubs to rear a pig and then share it out in winter.

"Everybody were into bottling! I mean, they were 'Digging for Victory' so everybody were growing fruit and vegetables and things. We used to buy these bottling jars and bottle tomatoes and fruit if you could get it, and salt kidney beans or runner beans. Y'know, you used to chop them up and put a layer of salt and then another layer of beans, another layer of salt. You used to do all these things so that you could have vegetables in winter."
HUDDERSFIELD WOMAN BORN 1915

"I can remember my father bottling plums, he always seemed to be bottling plums, all summer - it wouldn't be, but to me as a child he seemed to do that. And he used to put eggs in isinglass, you know, in big containers to keep them."
CLECKHEATON WOMAN BORN 1932

"Oh, lard was rationed as well, so quite a lot of people made pastry out of liquid paraffin. Sounds revolting doesn't it ..."
HUDDERSFIELD WOMAN BORN 1924

Now comes Part 5 *in the* POTATO PLAN

Use Potatoes in place of flour

(PART POTATOES, PART FLOUR)

Have you tried this latest addition to the Potato Plan? Here it is :
Use potatoes in place of part of the flour, when making pastry, puddings and cakes. The potatoes can be cooked the day before, if more convenient, and mashed while hot. Watch out for further recipes in this series.

POTATO PASTRY
Rubbing-in method. 4 ozs. mashed potatoes; 8 ozs. flour; 2 ozs. fat; ¼ teaspoonful salt. Mix flour and salt, rub in fat, then work into the potato. Mix to a stiff dough, with a small amount of cold water if necessary. Knead and roll out.
Creaming method. 4 ozs. mashed potatoes; 8 ozs. flour; 2 ozs. fat; ¼ teaspoonful salt. Cream fat and potato, add the flour. No moisture is necessary. Mix to a stiff dough and roll out.

The 4 other parts of the Plan
1 Serve potatoes for breakfast on three days a week.
2 Make your main dish a potato dish one day a week.
3 Refuse second helpings of other food. Have more potatoes instead.
4 Serve potatoes in other ways than "plain boiled."

Bread costs ships . . . Eat home-grown potatoes instead

ISSUED BY THE MINISTRY *MF* OF FOOD, LONDON, W.I.
P.22.

PRESERVES FROM THE GARDEN

"GROWMORE" BULLETIN No. 3 OF THE MINISTRY OF AGRICULTURE AND FISHERIES PUBLISHED BY HIS MAJESTY'S STATIONERY OFFICE PRICE 4d. NET

MAKING THE FAT RATION GO FURTHER

MINISTRY OF FOOD WAR COOKERY LEAFLET 19 Number

A wartime cookery book, Ministry of Food leaflet and newspaper recipe. A great number of such items were published to help and encourage the housewife to make the most of the limited food resources and substitutes.

"My wife's grandmother she used to entertain troops at home ... and she made some beautiful Robin cake. There was no fat to make Robin cake with - she used to use liquid paraffin ... it wasn't any good for exercises, you didn't run any better [non-laxative effect], but it was lovely cake, lovely cake! I can taste it now."
GOLCAR MAN BORN 1922

KITCHEN FRONT

"... during the Second World War I made butter every week. We had a mixer that mixed eggs and things, and I used to save the cream for a week and then make - I always did a quarter of butter every week, fresh butter, because my mother had been a farmer's daughter and she taught me how to do it, and I did it all the war, and it was lovely."
HUDDERSFIELD WOMAN BORN 1906

"We used to make us own truffles out of dried milk - well they didn't seem too bad. Made them sort of sweets during the war, cocoa seemed to be the main ingredient."
CLECKHEATON WOMAN BORN 1932

"... they used to mix some milk in with the butter which would thin it out so that it would spread a little bit further, so that we could try to have butter on our bread every day of the week."
MIRFIELD MAN BORN 1930

"... you got your milk in a jug then, not in a bottle - was delivered to your door - and you skimmed the cream off and you mixed it with margarine which was plentiful, and it made it taste a bit like butter, a little bit better than margarine was you know."
HUDDERSFIELD WOMAN BORN 1924

"I looked after someone's hens if they went away, so they gave me the eggs, so that was a great help. You could keep five hens if you had room for them, and you could have a ration of stuff - instead of the eggs - to feed them on."
HIGHTOWN WOMAN BORN 1919

"... the hens kept us supplied with eggs y'see. I mean, there was two or three eggs every day and then if we were short of anything, if a hen had given up laying, well I would wring its neck, pluck it and clean it and put it in the pot. The kids didn't mind the hens but y'see they'd more or less made pets of the rabbits ... We kept about five rabbits in t'back garden. But I didn't dare tell the kids it was their rabbits they were eating!"
HUDDERSFIELD WOMAN BORN 1902

Potato Carrot Pancake

Well-seasoned mashed potato combined with cooked carrot makes a wholesome and savoury-tasting pancake. Whip the mashed potato to a loose creamy consistency. Season well with pepper and salt and add some diced cooked carrot. Pan-fried slowly in a very little fat it develops a deliciously crisp crust, but it can be baked to a good brown in the oven if preferred.

Wartime recipe from a newspaper Ministry of Food information column.

"I used to go to the YM[CA] because I used to help there as well ... the soldiers used to come ... at night we'd be making sandwiches, and we were only allowed so much margarine, and we used to have to melt it and put it on with a paintbrush."
HUDDERSFIELD WOMAN BORN 1899

WAR-TIME COOKERY.
A CLASS of 12 weeks' duration will be held at the
TECHNICAL COLLEGE, Halifax Road, DEWSBURY,
on THURSDAYS (2-30—4),
Commencing on THURSDAY, 16th JANUARY.
FEE for the Course. 2s. 6d.   31724

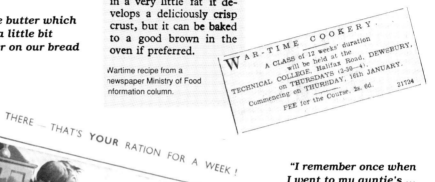

THERE — THAT'S YOUR RATION FOR A WEEK !

A "BAMFORTH" COMIC

"I remember once when I went to my auntie's ... I went to tea. [She said] 'Just warm that butter for me' and I was warming it in front of the fire in the dish you see, ooh and it slipped out. Ooh dear! - she wasn't really cross because she wasn't that type to be cross ... oh and I can fair see that butter drip-drop out you know, it had melted ... and she was scraping it all off - she didn't throw it away though!"
HUDDERSFIELD WOMAN BORN 1931

"... there was a great spirit of this, [sharing] I mean, I know it sounds a silly little thing now, but I can remember one of our neighbours being given a tin of evaporated milk, Carnation milk, as an extra, and she must have felt so guilty about it, that she brought it round to my mother, and gave half to us ... It was a real treat, was this."
HUDDERSFIELD MAN BORN 1931

KITCHEN FRONT

A variety of 'new' foods were introduced to bolster the meagre rations, many arriving on food shipments from America under the Lend-Lease agreement. Local people were delighted with American spam and sausagemeat, and even dried eggs were generally appreciated. Opinions varied greatly about the more unusual 'new' foods such as whalemeat and horsemeat, but many local people have said they ate and enjoyed both.

"... a real treat would be a tin of spam. There'd be a supply of tinned meat come in to the grocer's down at Batley Carr and each customer would be allowed maybe one tin ... I can remember thinking how marvellous it was, you know - the best food we'd had for ages and ages ..."
HUDDERSFIELD MAN BORN 1931

"My mother used to use this as a substitute for bacon. She used to fry it and it used to be quite nice, spam fried, I remember."
BATLEY MAN BORN 1926

"... you know the [dried] eggs were super scrambled. You reconstituted them and made scrambled eggs and they were really good!"
HUDDERSFIELD WOMAN BORN 1925

"You'd reconstitute it [dried egg] with so much water and beat it up ... and it was a yellow powder ... I made sponge cakes and fruit cakes - all sorts of things."
HIGHTOWN WOMAN BORN 1919

"In the canteen at work a great delicacy was whalemeat ... it was quite good, quite good. I wouldn't eat it now of course but it was quite good at the time and it was filling. It was very meaty, it didn't taste fishy, it tasted like meat."
GOLCAR MAN BORN 1922

Tins of dried eggs and dried milk from the United States. Under the Lend-Lease agreement with the United States, Britain could postpone payment for munitions and food until after the war.

"I remember coming home once and we thought this meat was beautiful and when we'd eaten it my mother said 'What did you think about that?' and we said 'Oh we thought it was lovely', and she said 'It was heart' and so we were all sick. And we said 'Don't get any more we'd rather not have any' and she said 'Well you really enjoyed it, you thought it was good'. The butcher had had this heart in but we decided that we didn't want it any more."
HUDDERSFIELD WOMAN BORN 1922

"During the war [in the fish shop] ... I think I cooked thirty or forty different kinds of fish - fish you never see now. They just got fish from anywhere. Some was nice, some came out like rubber!"
HUDDERSFIELD WOMAN BORN 1925

"My husband's mother used to get whalemeat and she used to bring us some, and horsemeat too. And the first time she brought it she didn't tell us what it was y'see, and of course we ate it - and we really enjoyed it! Then she told me what it was. Well, I felt then a bit as though 'Ugh, I can't eat that, I can't eat that' but we'd already eaten it y'see - so we kept on!"
HUDDERSFIELD WOMAN BORN 1902

"There was a horsemeat shop in town ... a lot of people wouldn't touch it, but a lot of people bought horsemeat to supplement their meat ration because it wasn't on ration wasn't horsemeat."
HUDDERSFIELD WOMAN BORN 1925

MAKE DO AND MEND

Many local women remember the slogan 'Make Do and Mend' and the challenges they faced in trying to clothe themselves and their families during the war. Although new clothes were available, they became increasingly expensive until they came under Government control with the Utility scheme from 1941-2. From June 1941 they became subject to rationing by a points system. Sixty-six coupons per year were allocated to each person; in 1942 it was cut to forty-eight. As an example, sixteen coupons were required for a man's coat, and fourteen for a woman's coat. Cloth and knitting wool also required coupons. It became second nature to dye and to alter, to cut down clothes for children, and to ingeniously change an items use. Clothes were made from any available material such as curtains, black-out material, army blankets and parachute silk. 'Make Do and Mend' classes were held at local Technical Colleges, and exhibitions mounted around the area with talks and demonstrations on how to make the most of existing clothing. The war created work for many, and for those wealthy enough to buy clothes, the limited coupon allowance was often frustrating. By contrast some people in Kirklees were too poor to take advantage of what clothing coupons they were issued with. Clothing coupons often illegally changed hands for money or other goods.

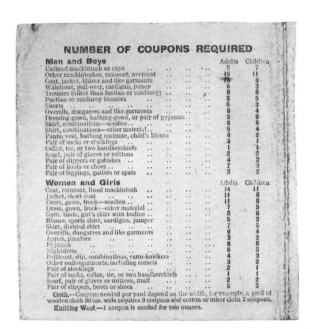

Wartime chart showing how many coupons were required for each item of clothing.

"Everything was mended and patched and darned and better mended y'know. It was made to last as long as possible."
HUDDERSFIELD WOMAN BORN 1915

"You had to make do, make things do. You had to mend, oh forever mending things and patching and I know that when he [husband] changed his job he got a little bit more money and I was able to spend a few coupons on some pants and vests and that was a luxury!"
HIGHTOWN WOMAN BORN 1919

IF YOU HAVEN'T ANY COUPONS, WHAT CAN YOU DO?

"The clothing as far as the younger end was concerned was really the worst thing. I mean, you see these nice things and for the first time in your life you had some money to spend but you couldn't get it 'cause you hadn't enough clothing coupons."
HUDDERSFIELD WOMAN BORN 1925 LAND GIRL

"Oh, I had no money - most people, poor people, had to sell their clothing coupons, and their sweet coupons. Because I had no money to buy clothes with - I'd no money for sweets at all - I was very poor ... I never bought clothes - I used to have things given or you could go to a jumble sale and get things - I couldn't afford clothes 'cause I'd never any money!"
HUDDERSFIELD WOMAN BORN 1916 SOLDIER'S WIFE

MAKE DO AND MEND

"You used to cut things down and make other things from them, so you might have had a dress that you cut the top off and just use the skirt part. You used to make slippers from, well, when I was in the Forces we used to make slippers from jeep cushions, I don't know where they'd come from, nobody enquired ... knitting wool of course was on ration and then it got to the stage where the yarn got coarser and coarser and ticklier and ticklier and you used to knit with this."
MIRFIELD WOMAN BORN 1923
ATS

"... pyjamas for children out of your hubby's old pyjamas, shirts the same, childrens blouses out of dad's stripey shirt tails which weren't worn - oh it was endless the things you did with sewing."
HUDDERSFIELD WOMAN BORN 1915

"Shaw & Hallas shoe shop along John William Street ... they used to get 'Joyce' shoes which were very famous shoes at that time, and they were low heels because during the black-out you couldn't teeter about on high heels really, 'cause you couldn't see where you were going. And they were very smart, low heeled ones and they looked nice. And so we used to put our names down for these 'Joyce' shoes, and when they got the stock in they used to send a postcard or something. And oh, we thought it was marvellous if we got a pair of 'Joyce' shoes!"
HUDDERSFIELD WOMAN BORN 1922

"While we were at Batley, I can remember that we did get new clothes at Whitsun, because my mother had saved money and coupons, and the church that we went to, they had a Whit walk up near Soothill. When I say new clothes, it was probably something like a new shirt and a jersey - it certainly wasn't a suit, 'cause we couldn't have afforded the money, never mind anything else. But yes, we did get new clothes at Whitsun, because it was part of the thing to do. And, well, it sounds daft really, that there was all sorts of standards being absolutely thrown out of the window, and yet there were other standards that you wouldn't dream of letting slip, you know - a bit like dressing for dinner in the jungle - I'm not suggesting Batley's a jungle!"
HUDDERSFIELD MAN BORN 1931
EVACUEE FROM HULL TO BATLEY

ONE CAN'T BLAME GIRLS FOR WORRYING ABOUT SILK STOCKINGS TO-DAY. WHAT HAPPENED TO THE GIRL WHO WORE COTTON ONES? WHY, NOTHING! I'VE HEARD THEM SAY!

A "BAMFORTH" COMIC

"Ladies stockings, generally, if they couldn't get silk - there were no nylon then - if they couldn't get silk or mercerised cotton they finished up with painted legs. They weren't wearing stockings, they were bare legs which were dyed. And I have memories of painting a seam down the back of me girlfriends legs because she wasn't wearing stockings and wanted people to think she was."
GOLCAR MAN BORN 1922

"... it looked quite effective, except sometimes when it rained, all your leg make up ran off down your leg!"
HUDDERSFIELD WOMAN BORN 1925

"... they were made of parachute material, one was in turquoise and one was in white and I think they were t'best petticoats I've ever had. They're still in service ... an old lady made 'em me, I got the material from an Air Force chap ..."
LIVERSEDGE WOMAN BORN 1910

Clothing Book 1943-44

Clothing coupons from a Clothing Book.

UTILITY

The Utility scheme was introduced by the Board of Trade in 1941-2. Its aims were to make the most of limited raw materials by standardising the production of goods, and to ensure that ordinary people could buy good quality clothing, furniture, shoes, bedding and household utensils at reasonable prices. Utility goods were restricted to specific materials and designs. The supply of these goods to the public was also controlled. Attitudes towards the Utility items varied. Many local people however could not afford to buy new goods, Utility or otherwise.

"I remember t'furniture were horrible. Clothing wasn't so bad but furniture were terrible. It were like orange boxes!"
HECKMONDWIKE WOMAN BORN 1926

"It was very good standard, very well made - much better that it is today. If it had a kite mark on - the Utility mark on - you could rely on it being good, but they were very plain. There were no frills, no fancy things about them."
HIGHTOWN WOMAN BORN 1919

"... it only had to have a certain number of buttons, it had to be very plain. You could have the skirts - you could have three pleats at the front and one at the back, but that was all. Shoulders at that time were quite coat-hangerish, very military looking really. Shoes were very plain, there were just a few styles in everything. Similarly, coats. Everybody wore hats of course ... and if you had things made, if you went to a dressmaker or a tailor, they were still only allowed to follow this set pattern."
MIRFIELD WOMAN BORN 1923

"Well personally I thought they were smart. They were made of as little material as possible of course ... we'd suits - I liked suits so I thought they looked exceedingly smart. This is when the skirts came up actually to the knee length to save on material. Fitted, really fitted jackets were made, more on the lines of uniform than anything ..."
HUDDERSFIELD WOMAN BORN 1924

"Utility - it created a new fashion did wartime clothing. They went from the wide sloppy trousers for men, with twenty-six [inch] bottoms, down to twenty-two - I think they finished up about seventeen. Turn-ups went ... Not only did the trousers suffer, everything seemed to get smaller, tighter - apart from ties. The wartime fashion for ties was broad ones, kipper ties ... the only way a man could express any fashion sense was in his ties. They were always big wide ones during wartime."
GOLCAR MAN BORN 1922

Document accompanying Utility 'Dockets' allowing the purchase of blankets and sheets which were in restricted supply.

The Utility mark CC41 (Civilian Clothing 1941) which appeared on all Utility goods.

"I remember a Utility bicycle and I remember this distinctly. In the place of the plated areas which normally would be nice and shiny, nicely chrome plated, it was sprayed black, it was all black, and another thing was that the pedals ... which before the war would have two rubber inserts, sort of non-slip inserts, because of the shortage of rubber they'd put in a wooden block, two wooden blocks. Overall it looked very drab and they'd utilised wood ... they'd utilise all kinds of materials to replace materials which were needed for war production."
BATLEY MAN BORN 1926

SHORTAGES

There were shortages of almost everything. The production of household articles such as razor blades and shoe polish was severely restricted as resources were directed towards war production. Most people simply had to do without. Shops would sometimes be supplied with quotas of scarce goods and long queues would form immediately. Wealthy and influential people often managed to acquire what they needed despite shortages and rationing.

The basic ration of petrol was abolished in 1942, and it was then restricted to those people authorised for work or health reasons. This led to a 'black market', as well as many prosecutions for its misuse. Local people were more affected by restrictions on public transport, such as reduced frequency and earlier last services. Shortage of coal was also a great problem - although not officially rationed the supply was very restricted.

"At the beginning of the war selfish people went out on a spending spree and of course the people who were better off were able to buy up all manner of tinned objects and have a cache of this in the same way as people went out getting hold of petrol, and keeping petrol, surreptitiously ..."
BATLEY MAN BORN 1926

"I think there was a very small ration [of petrol] but it was so small that I remember in 1940 Dad ran the car into the garage, and it was standing up on wooden blocks, the wheels off the ground, for the rest of the war. It just wasn't worth running it."
HIGHTOWN MAN BORN 1920

"You couldn't get lipsticks or face powder or anything like that but my husband knew a chemist and sometimes he used to bring me some face powder and some lipstick, but you couldn't get face creams much or anything like that because it was fat y'see."
HUDDERSFIELD WOMAN BORN 1899

WOULD LIKE TO COME AND SEE YOU, BUT I'M AFRAID THERE'S NO HOPE UNLESS WE COME LIKE THIS!

A bottle of 'Californian Poppy' perfume treasured since wartime. This was a very popular fragrance at the time.

"Stockings were another thing that was scarce and you'd to depend on some soldiers coming from France or somewhere with silk stockings. And they were terrible really. They were quite nice but you wouldn't wear them now you know, all odd colours ... they brought them you know for presents ... those that got into France."
HUDDERSFIELD WOMAN BORN 1899

As beautiful as a summer morning ...
as fresh as a mountain stream ...
as startling as a fanfare ...
as precious as a family heirloom ...

Californian Poppy

PERFUME

Such a big demand, such a restricted supply — means that someone sometimes may be disappointed. Sorry!

CAL 74-974-55   PROPRIETARY PERFUMES LTD.

SHORTAGES

"Well everybody sort of wanted cigarettes. I think there used to be horrible brand called Pasha's which were a Turkish brand that people had if there was nothing else. And certainly in Dewsbury at that time, when I used to be going to the library, there was a little tobacconist's - he used to get his quota of cigarettes in on a Thursday and people used to queue for them. He didn't believe in having things under the counter, he just wanted to get rid of them, and I used to go and queue there for cigarettes."
MIRFIELD WOMAN BORN 1923

"I remember sitting on the settee in front of the fire with a blanket, with my mother and father, with a blanket over us in the depths of winter to keep ourselves warm."
BATLEY MAN BORN 1926

"The one thing that I do remember in particular is the coldness in the war, being cold in the house ... it must have been shortage of fuel."
CLECKHEATON WOMAN BORN 1932

"... to make coal go further, 'cause coal was rationed you see, you used to sort of have coal bricks, and jam jars - put a jam jar on the fire you see, and stack these coal bricks round it and that gave off more heat, and it saved you your coal, made your coal go further."
DEWSBURY WOMAN BORN 1930

"Mother and my sister ... they used to go right up to Shaw Cross to get briquettes from the Colliery, to supplement the coal ration. And they were fairly heavy, and they had to make their way by bus which, from Gomersal to Shaw Cross wasn't the best journey - and carrying briquettes back!"
GOMERSAL MAN BORN 1928

"Our coal man had come to us the year before and said 'You ought to get some coal into your cellar' so I said 'Put as much as you can in', y'know ... and he filled a great big cellar from floor to ceiling with coal, lovely coal, that we could hardly open the door. Because you were only allowed two bags every month or two y'know. We were fortunate in that way that if we had any friends with children or who were very badly off for coal we didn't take the ration ... I'd say 'Well this month or two months let so-and-so have it y'see'."
HUDDERSFIELD WOMAN BORN 1899

CHEERIO! BET YOU CAN FIND A GOOD HOME FOR THIS! (SORRY I HAVEN'T A LEMON TO SEND AS WELL).

WHEN THEY RATIONED SOAP, WHY DIDN'T THEY MAKE A RIGHT JOB OF IT AND RATION WATER?

FINEST PRE-WAR SCOTCH WHISKY

"... pans were in short supply ... and me grandma had bought two enamel baby's potties because she couldn't get pans, so she cooked in the baby's potties - that sounds revolting, but they were clean, you know, I mean she'd a couple of iron pans, but no way could you replace an iron pan through the war ..."
HUDDERSFIELD WOMAN BORN 1924

BLACK MARKET

The 'black market' operated to some extent all over the country and Kirklees was no exception. Local people were clearly aware of it, and although a few say they had nothing at all to do with it, many others recall taking part in some small way, or talk of people whom they suspected did so.

"There used to be a saying regarding the black market - 'Under the counter'. In fact, customers would ask you 'What is under the counter?'."
HUDDERSFIELD MAN BORN 1927
SHOP WORKER

"Maybe three or four times a year with this general order of goods that we used to obtain from Headquarters there would be items which were called picnic hams ... but the Manager always seemed to take possession of those immediately for his so called 'special customers'."
HUDDERSFIELD MAN BORN 1927
SHOP WORKER

"Well, I think t'majority - everybody were in it. It were no secret. Everybody had a dabble in it somewhere and somehow, and what you don't get by fair means you got by false or foul. But as I say, there were once a chap - a Superintendent - found with a whole pig at t'back of his car and if that's not black market I don't know what is!"
LIVERSEDGE WOMAN BORN 1910
AUXILIARY POLICEWOMAN

"I used to go to the Monday market - and it was a secret then - and we got margarine coupons, and I used to buy bits of material to make night-dresses and that sort of thing and give them margarine coupons instead. They were worth a shilling each!"
HUDDERSFIELD WOMAN BORN 1899

"During the war that pig was sort of the illicit pig. You know, you'd a legal pig and an illicit pig. And every one of the neighbours would collect any crusts of bread, scraps, bit and pieces, and when that pig was killed there was a piece for everybody ... The Government knew about the other one, but this was - I suppose this is what's called the black market, but it was sufficiently innocent enough. It wasn't robbing anything from anybody else. Basically it was something to trade you see, because we used to trade one of the hindquarters of this pig with somebody at Hade Edge who happened to have sufficient on the side at their smallholding ... it was a form of primitive barter at that point of time and this pig was all part of it."
FARNLEY TYAS WOMAN BORN 1936
FARMER'S NIECE

"I can remember my father who was home on leave got the job of taking Uncle Walter's van up with all these pieces of pig all wrapped up and labelled for, you know, who they were for. And he's going on the way, and almost at the Bay Horse this policeman flags him down. He'd got a puncture on his bike. Well of course it was obvious what was in the van and as he [policeman] got out he took his bike off the top and he just held his hand out, and me father just put his hand in the back and gave him a parcel - he didn't know who's it was like! So I suppose that policeman had an illicit piece of pig on his Christmas table."
FARNLEY TYAS WOMAN BORN 1936
FARMER'S NIECE

"We had a shop in Cleckheaton and the upper echelons went there for all their groceries ... And they got the things that we didn't get. And I once saw some tinned fruit being handed over, and I said 'Can I have my ration of tinned fruit please?' He said 'But there isn't any ration' 'Oh yes' I said 'I've seen Mrs So-and-so get so-and-so and I've seen so-and-so' I said 'Is it all right if I go down to the Town Hall and ask about the ration?' So they gave me a tin of fruit that day. There was black market for those that had the money to pay for it!"
HIGHTOWN WOMAN BORN 1919

"... a butcher that we knew, he used to go during the night and pick a sheep up from somebody he knew who was prepared to let him have this sheep, and he killed it and he had some extra meat ... they weren't supposed to be doing that but he did do that. But he wasn't doing it for himself, he was doing it to try to help his customers 'cause he had such a little bit of stuff to sell them."
HUDDERSFIELD WOMAN BORN 1925

"I used to think it was not quite the thing, but I had good friends who did give me things. I'd people who had a public house and they would give me some butter or dripping, apples, oranges - but I knew where they'd come from, but I didn't ask. They'd come from the barracks and the soldiers brought them in in return for drinks."
HIGHTOWN WOMAN BORN 1919

"There was a shop in Dewsbury called J & B's ... if you came on leave and produced your paybook and what not, they would often let you have a pair of khaki silk stockings if they'd got them."
MIRFIELD WOMAN BORN 1923
ATS

"I think I brought the first pair of nylons into Huddersfield. I got nylons from the American airmen and brought 'em here and I could sell 'em. Well as you know there were a black market on anything during the war, and I was knocking about with some of these Yanks ..."
HUDDERSFIELD MAN BORN 1913
WAR WORKER, A V ROE'S, YEADON

THOUGHT THESE WOULD BE JUST UP YOUR STREET !
AND THEY'RE A GIFT TO-DAY THAT'S HARD TO BEAT.
COUPON-FREE, RIGHT TO YOUR DOOR—REALLY, WHAT COULD YOU WISH FOR MORE ?

1 DOZ PAIRS Fully-fashioned PURE SILK

IF YOU DON'T WANT IT, PLEASE RETURN IT—

I CAN GET A FIVER FOR IT ANY TIME !

"If I wanted some clothes I'd buy clothing coupons off somebody - these that had a load of kids, that couldn't afford to buy clothes. You'd a lot of second-hand stalls in those days, because people would buy second-hand things. But I used to buy clothing coupons, and I think all young people did because you couldn't get enough - I'd never enough clothing coupons."
HECKMONDWIKE WOMAN BORN 1926

"I got sweets on t'black market, I got dripping on t'black market, from t'fish shop, he let me have a pound of dripping now and again, and do you remember E... W... the footballer? He were my sweet man. He could always get sweets where nobody else could get them, and I always got them without coupons while I were in t'police force."
LIVERSEDGE WOMAN BORN 1910
AUXILIARY POLICEWOMAN

IF THE INVADER COMES

In 1940 there was a very real fear and expectation that Britain could be imminently invaded by the Germans, particularly after the fall of France in June when Britain stood alone. Paratroopers were especially feared and various measures were taken in each locality to combat and confuse any enemy troops who may have landed there. Here in Kirklees the Local Defence Volunteers (later Home Guard) were formed, and security measures taken such as removing or obliterating all signs which could identify this locality, or direct towards other localities, such as on streets, bus stops and buildings. Government leaflets told people what to do if invasion came.

There was also a fear of a 'Fifth Column' - sympathisers inside the country. Posters and leaflets emphasised the need to guard against 'Careless Talk'. In June 1940 the Government ordered people not to spread statements or rumours 'likely to cause alarm or despondency', under penalty of fine or imprisonment. Around the country 'aliens' were suspected as spies or potential collaborators and many were interned or had their movements restricted. Local people recall, often with amusement, some of the anti-invasion measures taken at this time.

Leaflet distributed by the Government to the public telling them what they should do if German troops invaded Britain

"It was a bit frightening really, because when they'd got to the French coast and Jersey ... only a mile or two away, it was frightening, yes. It made you wonder what you would do. Course and we'd leaflets to tell us what to do if they did invade."
HUDDERSFIELD WOMAN 1915

"A lot of the names were removed and they took it really, that side of it, to ridiculous limits because you'd have the local Co-op ... which would have something like 'The Batley and District Co-operative Society' on it and the 'Batley' had been removed, y'know, by the authorities. Now that was all right if it was on a board y'know, where it had been painted on -'BATLEY'. But in some cases, what you'd have is the individual letters, y'know, the 'B'-'A'-'T'-'L'-'E'-'Y', had been screwed on to the stone wall and they would still insist on these coming down. And when you took the brass letters or whatever it was off, obviously the mark where they'd been was still there, so you could still read it! ... but they just went through this ritual of removing all potential help, y'know, to anybody who landed. So that if German paratroopers had have landed in Batley they wouldn't have known whether they were in Batley or Dewsbury - and lots of signs were removed like this from public buildings."
HUDDERSFIELD MAN BORN 1931

"... carved in t'stone were Roberttown Council School and what they did ... they chiselled t'letters off!"
ROBERTTOWN MAN BORN 1912

IF THE INVADER COMES

"This is the ridiculous thing - if anybody asked, somebody told you kindly didn't they. I mean, they'd give you directions! If you were a German spy you'd say 'Oh what's the way to so and so?' 'Oh it's such and such and such' - they'd tell you where you were! So I mean it was a bit pointless was that road sign thing."
HUDDERSFIELD WOMAN BORN 1925

"On one occasion I and two friends were out for a Sunday afternoon's cycling, and we went out to Ilkley. Now at this time one was likely to come across a road block in the middle of a road. This was a brick wall which was built across half the road, and there was a sort of sentry box, and there were soldiers on duty there who would stop anybody suspicious. This was built at the time when we expected to have an invasion force in the country. All kinds of anti-invasion measures were taken. Fields, any prospective landing grounds were filled with all kinds of - wrecked and junked cars were put in, all kinds of stakes were driven in, wires to stop any landing of aircraft or gliders for airborne troops and also many of the roads had these road blocks. So we were out this Sunday and we came upon this road block ... I was a member of the local model aircraft club and used to go out to various venues to fly and in fact we had model boxes with us, we were going to fly, and we were stopped and they were very suspicious - what had we in the boxes?"
BATLEY MAN BORN 1926

BB 9aa (GB 6) Einzelobjekte:

✚	Lazarett, Krankenhaus
⚒	Eisengießerei
⊛	Chemisches Werk
♟	Wasserwerk, Hochbehälter
⬗	Wasserwerk, Erdbehälter
▭	Kläranlage, Abwässerwerk
⬤	Textilindustrie
⬥	Textilwaren
⬚	Ziegelei
⋈	Eisenbahnbrücke
≍	Straßenbrücke
—	Fußgängerbrücke, Steg
⌄	Schleuse
‖	Kanalüberführung
⁙	Wehr ohne Übergangsmöglichkeit

"... what I wrote to my husband was censored and what he sent to me was censored, and they used to black them out if you'd mentioned a place name or anything. So you used to have little codes where you could write things so that nobody but you knew what they meant. It might have been something about - well, when he was going abroad and he sailed from Liverpool ... he said something so that I would know that it was Liverpool but nobody else would."
MIRFIELD WOMAN BORN 1923

Section from the 'Stadtplan von Huddersfield'. British Ordnance Survey maps had been obtained by the Germans. This one of Huddersfield, overprinted in German, marked points of military significance such as chemical works, railway bridges and waterworks.

Wartime trolley bus tickets. No opportunity was wasted for getting wartime appeals across to the public.

"There were all these slogans on the war - 'Careless Talk Costs Lives' - and people used to take notice of 'em as well. You'd sit in a bus and you'd see this notice, great big ones in black and red I think they were, 'Careless Talk Costs Lives' and it were just as if a zip fastener went across your mouth for a few minutes."
HUDDERSFIELD WOMAN BORN 1926

HOME GUARD

The fear of enemy invasion led to the formation of the Local Defence Volunteers (soon renamed Home Guard) in May 1940. All available men between seventeen and sixty-five years old were asked in a public broadcast by Anthony Eden, Minister of War, to enrol to defend their neighbourhood, particularly against German paratroopers. Queues of volunteers formed immediately in Kirklees. These local men, many in reserved occupations who worked long hours during the day, spent long nights on patrol and gave up their days off to go on manoeuvres. Some people were amused by the activities of the Home Guard, but others believed it would have had some, if limited, success against German invaders.

"I volunteered for the Home Guard the second day after it was formed, got me name down. And I was pleased to be in the Home Guard. I was proud of being in the Home Guard. I couldn't go in the Forces so I went in the Home Guard."
GOLCAR MAN BORN 1922
HOME GUARD

"I've got to join something, and I didn't particularly fancy the Fire Service, and so this opportunity came along and I jumped as did literally thousands and thousands of other people. I mean there were people like my age, who were expecting to be called up, and there were veterans of the First World War who more or less answered the call ... it was very very simple, you were told if you wanted to join, go to your local police station, and I went and there was a queue stretching for yards and yards - chaps wanting to register."
HIGHTOWN MAN BORN 1920
HOME GUARD

"... one night a week I'd to be on duty so I left work at half-past seven, went home, wash, shave, changed, went up to Home Guard for about half-past eight and stayed there while half-past six in the morning and then came home. Wash, shave, changed, had breakfast and off to work you see, and we'd to do that once a week. Now during the week there was an evening training with the Home Guard if you weren't working over, and Sunday mornings, if you weren't working, you'd to go on Home Guard Sunday mornings as well."
HUDDERSFIELD MAN BORN 1915
HOME GUARD

B Company 26 Battalion West Riding Home Guard, Huddersfield

"There was the LDV ... a kind of semi-military organisation without uniform, virtually without weapons. All you got to signify that you were in fact a bona fide member of this organisation was a khaki armband with LDV written on it that they dished out to say that you were allowed to carry a shovel to bray the German on the head with you see ... there was no rifles in those days, in the very early days ... and as time went on we were promoted to be allowed to carry rifles around and eventually we were issued with army uniforms just to make us look like soldiers."
HUDDERSFIELD MAN BORN C.1922
HOME GUARD

"... we were expecting attack by paratroops and they set up observation posts. Well this part of the country was ideal because there were, from the days of the collieries, there were spoil heaps all over the place."
HIGHTOWN MAN BORN 1920
HOME GUARD

HOME GUARD

"There was a time when we were getting quite a number of night air raids up here, when we did fire-watching duties for the ARP people ... I'd been out I think every night that week fire-watching, and it was a cold night. There was a bit of a wind blowing and I got in the lee of the Old Pack Horse Inn y'know, greatcoat snuggled up, and I fell asleep. Standing up against the wall, leaning against the wall I fell asleep. Well of course in the army, I mean, that is a heinous crime. But the platoon officer - he sort of watched me grow up from being a boy, neighbour - he woke me up. He said 'Come on lad, let's have you off home'. And he walked me across that road - I just lived across the road from the Old Pack Horse - knocked on the door, mother came to the door, he said 'Mrs ... put this lad to bed, he's falling asleep standing on his feet' and that was that!"
HIGHTOWN MAN BORN 1920
HOME GUARD

"I was in C Company, 35 Battalion, West Riding Home Guard - we were supposed to guard Scapegoat Hill to keep it free from Germans ... We had at Scapegoat Hill to take a telephone message on the hour every hour. We were stationed at the Noddle Farm. The nearest telephone, public telephone box, was three-quarters of a mile down the road. We used to have to walk down the road to take this phone call, if there was one. It was to let us know if the Germans were invading. Evidently they were only allowed to invade on the hour, every hour!"
GOLCAR MAN BORN 1922
HOME GUARD

I DON'T AGREE WITH THEM PUTTING THESE OLD SWEATS ON HOME SERVICE;—I'VE NEVER HAD MY BACK WARM SINCE MY OLE MAN WENT!

In the years when our Country was in mortal danger
F. THOMAS
who served 11 Jul. 1940 - 31 Dec. 1944.
gave generously of his time and powers to make himself ready for her defence by force of arms and with his life if need be.
George R.I.
THE HOME GUARD

Home Guard Certificate and Defence Medal.

"My father was in the Home Guard ... of course they were mostly old soldiers from the First World War or young men who were not of an age to go into the Forces, and I mean they really enjoyed it you know, they really enjoyed it. Every so often on a Sunday you might just sort of go out into the garden and you'd see a head pop up you know from behind a wall with a tin hat on, and then there'd be another one popping up from behind another wall - 'Oh bloody Home Guard they're here again' - they were on manoeuvres all over you know. They thoroughly enjoyed it, they really did. They did a good job you know ... you never doubted but that they wouldn't be efficient you know, if the time came."
HUDDERSFIELD WOMAN BORN 1925

HOME GUARD

"... up by Deer Hill, we did our manoeuvres up there. And at the end of the night ... we were told 'Right manoeuvres is over' and we adjourned to t'White House pub where we used to have a gill and then make our way back to the drill hall, hand in our rifles and we considered we'd had a good time on these manoeuvres. It was a good night out. Kept us occupied."
GOLCAR MAN BORN 1924
HOME GUARD

"... very early on we just got the rifles and the ammunition, and there was virtually no tuition in firing a rifle - you just got down and did your best, sort of thing."
HIGHTOWN MAN BORN 1924
HOME GUARD

"... if they'd come straight away we were ill prepared. Later on we progressed into quite a respectable fighting unit ... Yes, later on we'd have put a fight up. We'd have given 'em something."
GOLCAR MAN BORN 1922
HOME GUARD

"I got into conversation with a Corporal ... he said 'You in a reserved occupation?' I said 'Well, so far, yes. Mind you I don't know how long I'll be, you know.' He said 'What are you doing?' I said 'Well don't laugh, I'm in the Home Guard.' He said 'I don't laugh mate. By gum, I take my hat off to you blokes' he said. 'You work all day, then learn to be a soldier at night. I wouldn't want that'. And you know he was quite genuine about this, I was really overcome by it."
HUDDERSFIELD MAN BORN 1920
HOME GUARD

51st Battalion West Riding Home Guard.
Note the two boys marching alongside them.

"... they were all, you know, like my father sort of thing. But they were a real cheery bunch. We had a tremendous amount of fun out of all this, despite the fact, as I say, that it was one gigantic bluff - and it might have paid off, I don't know."
HIGHTOWN MAN BORN 1920
HOME GUARD

HERE IS THE NEWS

Civilians avidly followed the progress of the war through newspapers, radio news and cinema newsreels. Throughout the war the nine o'clock news was the great event of the day. Some people had maps on their wall in which they stuck pins marking the progress of troops. However war news was heavily censored by the Government Ministry of Information, so as to give no information to the enemy. There was little news of German air raids - local newspapers wrote only of the bombing of 'a north-eastern town' with no identification. British propaganda exaggerated successes and understated losses in an effort to boost civilian morale.

"... everything stopped for the news. If you were somewhere, y'know you might have been visiting somebody or something - if it was time for the news, the news came on."
HUDDERSFIELD WOMAN BORN 1925

They always gave out favourable figures, I noticed that. We were always winning, even when we weren't. They never let us see the dark side, and there was a dark side naturally. But we were always winning - we'd always sunk more ships than they'd sunk; we'd always shot more planes down than they'd shot down; we'd always dropped more bombs than they'd dropped - on the German cities than they'd dropped here."
GOLCAR MAN BORN 1922

"... a thing which in later years has astonished me is that at a time when in the south of England the war in the air was being fought, the battle in the air which would make the difference between us being invaded and not being invaded, all this was going on - literally a life-and-death struggle - down there ... And we up here, at least to my recollection, knew nothing about this through the summer of 1940."
BATLEY MAN BORN 1926

German propagandists were also hard at work attempting to demoralise the British people. Perhaps the best known was Lord Haw Haw, who was popularly rumoured to have made many statements which implied the Germans had detailed knowledge of specific localities in Britain.

"THE LUFTWAFFE SHOT DOWN TEN R.A.F. BOMBERS!— ONE OF OUR TOWNS IS MISSING!"

DON'T HELP HAW-HAW.

Batley M.P. Attacks Rumour Mongers.

DANGERS OF WHISPERED "SECRETS."

Lord Haw Haw might be a most amusing radio personality, but he is a dangerous person, and, believe it or not, you can help him.

Captain Hubert Beaumont, M.P. for Batley, Morley and Ossett, believes so and, addressing a crowded Batley Hick Lane Brighter Black-out meeting on Sunday, he appealed to the public not to assist the Nazi broadcaster by being a rumour-monger.

Captain Beaumont congratulated the

"We listened to the German propaganda broadcasts as well. We weren't forbidden to listen to them. There was one famous one, William Joyce, who was known as Lord Haw Haw, he was a traitor, and his broadcasts we listened to them quite regularly. He used to come on - 'Germany calling, Germany calling' - and I can hear him now! I can hear his voice just as it was, and he always claimed stupendous victories for them. I think he broadcast about three times that they'd sunk the Ark Royal - three times before they eventually did sink it! He was a known propagandist and nobody took him seriously."
GOLCAR MAN BORN 1922

"I never actually heard him, but they always said that he made a reference to this area that they were going to bomb the mill where the name of the mill was on the chimney, and that was Burnley's [Gomersal]."
GOMERSAL MAN BORN 1928

"... By t'sound o' him he'd blown England to bits - there were nowt left standing! It were all propaganda ... it were a laugh. But he'd a peculiar voice, I don't know how to describe it - a sort of persuasive voice ... he was very persuasive. But nobody took no notice. You used to have a good laugh on a morning - what he'd been saying."
ROBERTTOWN MAN BORN 1912

ATTITUDES

Bamforth's wartime comic postcards depicted Hitler and his associates as figures of ridicule. Undoubtedly the attitudes of many people towards the enemy were partly shaped by British media propaganda, but must also have depended on how the war affected them personally. The full horror of the Nazi atrocities which influenced many people's views was not revealed until after the war. It is difficult for people to recall attitudes of so long ago, especially with the effect of hindsight, but local people have tried to describe how they felt towards the enemy during the war.

"Most of the Germans, they were very nice people ... We met with prisoners of war at this Taylor Hill Camp. They talked to us quite a lot and they said that they was all against it except the Nazis, and it was them that was causing all the bother."
HUDDERSFIELD WOMAN BORN 1902

"I didn't know there was prisoner of war camp up Taylor Hill till they started bringing them down [to dances at Greenhead Park]. They used to bring them in a van and they parked by the tent like. They went home - they was taken home - before the dance finished because our lads wouldn't come in. The lads that was at home wouldn't come in the nights that they was there y'see. So they was always taken, and then when they'd gone the lads would come in, after they'd gone."
HUDDERSFIELD WOMAN BORN 1902

"We got on very well with them [prisoners of war] except for these that they said was Nazis and they could be very, very nasty and they could say nasty things ... they had to sit around more than anything 'cause the girls were all warned not to dance with them. And if they wanted to dance they danced amongst themselves. The girls was told not to - oh some of 'em would y'know, take a risk and dance with them."
HUDDERSFIELD WOMAN BORN 1902

BY GUM, LAD, I WISH I'D HITLER HERE JUST NOW!

A "BAMFORTH" COMIC

"In my experience there was no line drawn between the leaders and the people - they were Germans, so they were bad. That was the attitude."
HUDDERSFIELD WOMAN BORN 1925

"It might not have been intentional but we were all brainwashed. There was no such thing as a good German. If a person was a German then obviously he was bad, and if he was an Italian he was obviously bad."
HUDDERSFIELD MAN BORN 1931

IF THIS WERE HITLER!

↓

WHAT WOULD YOU DO CHUMS?

"... we didn't dislike the Germans actually - none of us disliked the Germans, and me dad always used to say, 'It isn't the Germans, it's the Nazis' - it wasn't the Germans that were horrible, it were the Nazis. Y'know, the Germans had to fight like our lads had to fight, whether they wanted to or not. They were called up and they'd to go fight and that was it, same as the Germans had - they hadn't a choice."
HECKMONDWIKE WOMAN BORN 1926

"... the Germans belonged to somebody, somebody loved them didn't they ... They were somebody's sons, they were somebody's husbands and this is how - I still feel like this now, I've never altered my opinion, that whatever colour or creed you are, whatever denomination you are, you are a person ..."
HUDDERSFIELD WOMAN BORN 1924

"I don't think they realised until after the war how bad it had been y'know, with the persecution of the Jews and things like that."
HUDDERSFIELD WOMAN BORN 1920

"I'm not sure that 'hate's' the right word - dislike, and a lot of derision ... I think this is how a lot of people saw it. But I can't honestly think that we hated Hitler ... not violently. Not until after the war. I think it was the end of the war that - probably I was getting older ... and maybe understood it a bit more, and I think one of the most traumatic experiences was the revelation of the concentration camps ... once the photographs of Belsen and things like this were published then, yes, I think there was a feeling of hatred."
HUDDERSFIELD MAN BORN 1931

IF ONLY HE'D BEEN MARRIED TO THE RIGHT WOMAN!

THE GOOD OLD DAYS!

Patriotism was a strong attitude in the Second World War, but some people's memories indicate that 'joining up' was not necessarily done for patriotic reasons.

"I lived at home until the end of 1939, when I volunteered to join the Forces. There was no particular desire to be loyal to the country, but I think the real feeling was all my friends had either been called up, or two or three of them which were in the Territorial Army had had to go and commence their service for the war years in the August or the September when war was declared."
HUDDERSFIELD MAN BORN 1916

HAVE THOSE NAUGHTY BOMBERS GONE, HERMAN?

"I think probably most people - young lads of my generation - we didn't know what it was about and it was exciting. We'd been fed upon all this business about the glory of combat and all that nonsense you see ... we'd been brought up on the various comics and so forth, on the 'Dandy' and the 'Beano' and all these larger-than-life heroes there. And most of us too had gone into work which was not interesting, it was boring work and I think many people - young people who jumped the gun and didn't wait for actual call-up, but volunteered - I suspect that many of them volunteered simply to get away from a sort of mundane day to day set up."
BATLEY MAN BORN 1926

DIGGING FOR VICTORY

Shortages of imported food, and imported feed for livestock, led to a major national campaign for increased home food production. Farmers had to plough up as much land as possible to help reduce the need for food imports, and mechanisation was rapidly and widely introduced to increase output. The Women's Land Army and eventually thousands of German and Italian prisoners of war also worked on the farms.

On an individual level people were urged to 'Dig for Victory'. Many local people responded willingly as this was a way to supplement

their rigid diets with fresh fruit and vegetables as well as to 'do their bit' for the war effort. Allotments were created all around Kirklees, and gardens, school playing fields and public parks were also cultivated. Local 'Dig for Victory' exhibitions were a feature of the campaign with photographs of local Land Army girls, demonstrations of food preserving, and talks on poultry and rabbit feeding. The Spenborough 'Dig for Victory' campaign organised by the Allotments Committee encouraged allotment holding and special half size plots at 2s. 6d. per annum were advertised for 'ladies and young persons'.

Gardening Lecture At Gomersal.

Valuable Hints On Manuring.

The uses of various manures and how they should be applied in a war-time garden were lucidly explained by Mr. N. S. English in the first of a series of lectures to members of the Gomersal Gardeners' Association at the Gomersal Public Hall on Tuesday.

He said this was a time when we were all wanted to get more from our gardens and allotments, and there was considerably less manure available. The first important thing was digging. They never

"Of course there was the slogan 'Dig for Victory' and people who'd never shoved a spade in the ground before took allotments and that - tried to grow their own vegetables and all that sort of thing. My Father did. He had a very busy war, dad had. He was working, they were converted on to - well they were actually making lathes there and he was very busy there; he was in the Auxiliary Fire Service, and he also had this allotment where he used to grow celery and cabbages and potatoes."
HIGHTOWN MAN BORN 1920

"... one of our teachers in Batley had an allotment which I think belonged to the school ... but he used to take us down a group at a time to dig on this allotment and plant things, and the crops used to be sold to the children."
HUDDERSFIELD MAN BORN 1931

DIGGING FOR VICTORY

"I was 'Digging for Victory'. I'd an allotment about a mile away from home ... we grew vegetables for our own home use. I used to come off nights and call in the garden half an hour or an hour, dig a few vegetables up and bring them up for me mother and her neighbours. And they tasted good - you grew 'em yourself."
GOLCAR MAN BORN 1922

"Anybody with a largish garden would not be expected to be growing flowers, they would be expected to grow edible produce to try to, you know, help the campaign ..."
HUDDERSFIELD MAN BORN 1931

"Of course they wanted more production on the farm y'see, and fields was ploughed up. Fields that we'd never ploughed up before were starting to be ploughed up to grow corn for the war effort y'see. And there used to be men come from the Ministry of Agriculture to tell you what to do and what not to do, and which field to plough and which not, and what varieties to grow - all out effort to grow food y'see."
DENBY DALE MAN BORN 1922
FARMER

LIFE'S PAINFUL ONE WAY AND ANOTHER, AND OH BOY, DON'T WE KNOW IT! SEEMS TO ME IF WE WANT MORE GRUB WE'VE GOT TO BLINKIN' WELL GROW IT!

"DIG FOR VICTORY."

EASTER.

MAKE IT A GARDENING HOLIDAY.

PLANT POTATOES FOR VICTORY.

(By "HORTUS.")

Gardeners, of every size and kind of plot, from newly-turned lawns to market gardens, must contribute their share of potatoes to next year's winter store. The country expects it. We must not let anything interfere with a maximum effort. Easter, coming this year in mid-April, can be a potato planting holiday. Potatoes are de-

I'M DIGGING FOR VICTORY, AS YOU CAN SEE! WHY DON'T YOU CULTIVATE A PATCH, LIKE ME?

D. TEMPEST

"The wasting of food was considered very, very serious. Somewhere up near the Batley Rugby League ground, Mount Pleasant, there was a field up there that had been planted with wheat, and somebody had walked through it as it was almost ready for cutting. And there was a big outcry of trying to find who'd done it, because it had wasted this food."
HUDDERSFIELD MAN BORN 1931

"Everybody's working for that sort of war effort ... and y'know people would say 'Have you got your harvest in?' willing to give you a hand y'know."
DENBY DALE MAN BORN 1922
FARMER

FUND RAISING

Everyone had the opportunity to feel that they were helping to win the war by contributing to the war effort in some way. In towns and villages throughout Kirklees ordinary people raised great amounts of money through investment during the various special Government 'Savings Weeks' such as 'Wings for Victory' and 'Salute the Soldier'. Each area had its own target and each target had a purpose. During Warship Week in Huddersfield, one third of the target of £1,500,000 - the cost of a cruiser - was reached on the first day! In 1941 Heckmondwike broke the national record for the highest savings per head in 'War Weapons Week' by subscribing £42.7s.0d per head of population - the total collected was £364,147.10s. Dewsbury's 'Wings For Victory' target of £400,000, the cost of eight Halifax bombers and sixteen single-engined fighters, was raised to £600,000 as the savings poured in. The drive to raise enough money by donation to buy a Spitfire to be named after your town also caught local peoples imagination. These weeks were filled with special events such as exhibitions of military equipment, dances and whist drives. There was a strong element of competition between local areas to achieve the largest sums.

"... in one of these 'Wings for Victory' weeks I remember a German fighter, an Me 109, was displayed in Batley Market place ... By this time I was in the Air Training Corps ... I remember being set to guard this aircraft from the general public who were pushing and prodding and kicking at it and so forth, and I remember looking at it and thinking how incongruous it seemed to have this German fighter aircraft standing in a cobbled market place of a little West Riding woollen town."
BATLEY MAN BORN 1926

FUND RAISING

"... in the upper market at Heckmondwike they would have a Spitfire ... and you could go down and look at that. And of course the idea was that you all donated something so's that we could buy another Spitfire ... they used to have like a scale outside the Town Hall showing what we were achieving ... people used to donate and have little 'do's' to get cash together and see how much we could get."

GOMERSAL MAN BORN 1928

"In the early days of the war Batley raised - I think this was a magnificent effort - Batley raised the sum of £5,000, because this was the rate at which Spitfires were produced, this was the cost of mass producing Spitfire fighters - £5,000. And we in Batley by gift we produced enough money to buy a Spitfire."

BATLEY MAN BORN 1926

"... during these 'Weeks', you would have special lessons at school ... an obvious one would be the art lesson. You'd all be encouraged to paint aeroplanes, or ships, or whatever was in vogue at that time. But also, other lessons were directed towards those projects ... in the geometry or maths classes we were doing naval flags for signalling, and things like this ..."

HUDDERSFIELD MAN BORN 1931

The Spitfire aircraft 'Presented to the Nation from Contributions Received from the Public of Batley' to the Mayor's Spitfire Fund. The cheque for £5,000 illustrated here was presented to Lord Beaverbrook in October 1940, and a further cheque for £1,552 was presented in March 1941.

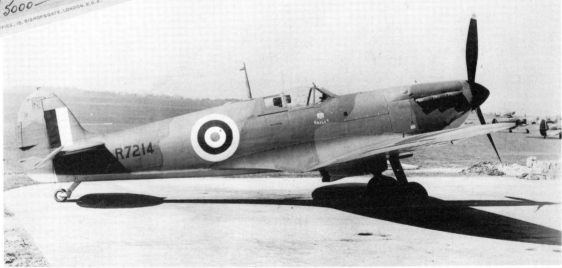

Supermarine Spitfire Mk. 1, R7214, 'BATLEY' was allocated to only one front-line operational unit - No 132 Squadron, RAF Peterhead - for only two months from 9 July 1941 to 10 September 1941. It then had to be repaired and became a maintenance instruction aircraft. In 1942 it was shipped out to the Middle East, where it ended its service 'career' on 27 July 1944.

BEATING THE SQUANDER BUG

Local people were urged through posters, leaflets and newspapers to help win the war by saving and conserving money, water, valuable fuel supplies, and resources such as public transport whose services were reduced due to fuel shortages. The 'Squander Bug' was the symbol of the National Savings Movement, whose message was to save rather than spend, thus lending money to the Government. This served as a uniting force as savings groups were organised in places such as schools and factories. Local people were urged to form street savings groups and many were established around Kirklees. Yet once again it should be remembered that many local people had no money to 'squander', and conserving resources was already a way of life.

"IT'S HARD WHEN A FELLOW'S SLIPPING OUT AND HIS WIFE LOOKS UP AND SAYS—"IS YOUR JOURNEY REALLY NECESSARY, JOE?"

"It got while that was a standing joke at the Palace [cinema] because if anyone got up to go to the toilet the comedian 'd be sure to say 'Is your journey really necessary?' and get a good laugh out of it".
GOLCAR MAN BORN 1922

The Squander Bug.

Huddersfield Corporation advertisement encouraging local people to save fuel.

ARE YOU HELPING TO
SAVE FUEL?

ECONOMISE WHENEVER POSSIBLE
LOOK ABOUT YOUR INSTALLATION
EACH UNIT SAVED IS OF VALUE
CHECK YOUR METERS EVERY WEEK
TURN OFF HEATERS WHEN NOT REQUIRED
REDUCE WASTE WATER IN KETTLES
ILLUMINATE ONLY WHEN REQUIRED
COOKERS SHOULD BE KEPT CLEAN
IS YOUR CYLINDER WELL LAGGED
THINK ABOUT THESE POINTS, FOR
YOUR COUNTRY NEEDS YOUR HELP

For further information apply to :

HUDDERSFIELD CORPORATION
ELECTRICITY DEPARTMENT
MARKET STREET.

Telephones :
3000-1-2-3 :4 lines ;

Engineer and Manager
E. LUNN, M.I.E.E.

"We were also exhorted to, when we took a bath, only to have 'x' number of inches of water, four inches of water or whatever it is, in order to save fuel."
BATLEY MAN BORN 1926

"The depth, if I remember rightly, was five inches - Yes, and we used to get in after each other - And a brick or something like that in your lavatory cistern so that you didn't take a full cistern full every time ... but in fact, to be quite honest, for a greater part of the war we didn't even have a running bath - we had one in front of the fire. Home comforts!"
GOMERSAL MAN BORN 1928 AND CLECKHEATON WOMAN BORN 1932

"I never squand - ered owt to tell you t'truth, because I had nothing. I couldn't afford to. That's what I say about t'war, you didn't squander owt because you couldn't afford to squander it - not if you did right."
LIVERSEDGE WOMAN BORN 1910

"I was brought up to save gas and electricity anyway for economies sake so we shouldn't be extravagent that way anyway."
HUDDERSFIELD WOMAN BORN 1915

"... posters with this horrible leering hairy thing which would incite a rather weak willed woman or man to spend up on this, that and the other rather than to put it into National Savings ... I remember a slogan for National Savings - 'Put your shirt on England - let's see you in-vest' which is a typical, a typical one."
BATLEY MAN BORN 1926

VOLUNTARY EFFORTS

Many local women, whether conscripted into war work or not, volunteered their time and energy towards the war effort, for example helping at first aid posts, hospitals or the YMCA, or taking troops or evacuees into their homes. Some made their contribution through the Womens Voluntary Service (WVS) - raising money for War Comforts Funds, organising homes for evacuees, and being ready to help the homeless after air raids. Women all around Kirklees knitted garments for the Forces, many forming into social knitting groups. By September 1941 the Mayoress of Batley's War Comforts Fund Committee reported that 20,413 knitted garments had so far been sent to Batley and Birstall men serving in the Forces.

"I can remember my mother being in a knitting party. Everybody was knitting you see for the soldiers and sailors and what not. And I can remember them all sitting round on a Monday afternoon, and they made the tea in turn. And I can remember the room in there being full of ladies all sitting round knitting like mad when I got home from school."
KIRKHEATON WOMAN BORN 1921

"I used to knit scarves, gloves, socks and [balaclava] helmets - I couldn't knit by pattern, I used to knit it out of my head."
HUDDERSFIELD WOMAN BORN 1916

"... we had a Comforts Fund in Kirkheaton and we used to go round to every house asking for a penny. And we used to have a box in the pubs, and they were very good - they used to collect quite a nice sum of money for us ... and that enabled us to send money or socks or things like that to the soldiers from Kirkheaton."
KIRKHEATON WOMAN BORN 1902

"My mother was in the WVS and she ran the savings group in the area, and every so often she'd have a whist drive in aid of funds. And she always provided things like cheese - 'cause we never ate all our ration - for prizes, and dripping from the [fish] shop. Y'see we had an allocation of fish and an allocation of dripping, but she always gave maybe a pound or something like that and people were really grateful if they won, if they got this ... She covered a substantial area round here ... and anyone in those streets who were in the Forces used to get a postal order ... that's where the funds basically went."
HUDDERSFIELD WOMAN BORN 1925

"... they wanted voluntary workers and with my husband being out all day I went to the First Aid Post - it was round in St. James' Road - from ten o'clock to five o'clock two days a week, and then I also went to the Infirmary - which was in Portland Street - from two o'clock to eight o'clock, just washing the patients and cleaning them up and that sort of thing."
HUDDERSFIELD WOMAN BORN 1899

SALVAGE

Due to shortages of raw materials the salvage of various items for re-cycling for the war effort became a way of life. It was also another way for the Government to focus public support and boost morale. Lord Beaverbrook, Minister of Aircraft Production, appealed to the 'women of Britain' to give up their aluminium pots and pans to provide metal to build more aeroplanes and local people responded willingly. The compulsory removal of iron railings though is recalled with some annoyance. Items that would normally be considered waste such as paper, cardboard and bones, were collected towards the war effort. It became an offence to throw away things such as rag, rope or string.

Large scale salvage 'drives' took place locally, and strong competitiveness for high achievement was again evident between towns and districts. In 1942 Meltham Urban District won the first prize of £500 in the Yorkshire area in a national waste paper salvage drive, when in one month the total amount of paper salvaged in the country was 100,000 tons.

"They wanted all your aluminium pans and that sort of thing and I had quite a lot but they were quite old. So I just turned them all in and went - you could buy any amount in the shops - and I bought a whole set of pans and I've still got some ... I had to because I hadn't any pans!"
HUDDERSFIELD WOMAN BORN 1899

"All the iron railings in the park was all taken down and never used ... They took them down 'cause they wanted the iron for munitions but they was all left for scrap ... It was a shame that they took the railings down ... the park gates used to be closed, locked at nine o'clock. It caused a lot of trouble y'know, people going in and sleeping in the park at night."
HUDDERSFIELD WOMAN BORN 1902

"... they never used them, and all these lovely gates and iron work and everything were all piled up as rubbish after the war. It was a shame."
HUDDERSFIELD WOMAN BORN 1899

"Every street had a food bin, a metal bin in the street and you put your food scraps in. I mean you never threw anything away. All your bits of scraps went to the food bin and that was collected regularly and that went to feed pigs."
HUDDERSFIELD WOMAN BORN 1925

"... you'd to save your paper and your waste and everything which we did, but if we'd any woollies or anything like that we used to save it and take it up to this mill. It mightn't be much but we thought it were as well us getting t'money than t'rag and bone man that came round. We could always get money for woollies."
HECKMONDWIKE WOMAN BORN 1926

Huddersfield schoolchildren collecting aluminium for the war effort.

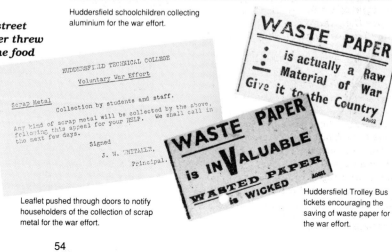

Leaflet pushed through doors to notify householders of the collection of scrap metal for the war effort.

Huddersfield Trolley Bus tickets encouraging the saving of waste paper for the war effort.

WORKING FOR WAR

The resource of labour was recognised as vital to success in the war. The whole of the population and industry were totally organised and directed towards the war effort, the aim being to ensure that 'each citizen is so engaged to make maximum use of his/her ability within the limits of the war economy'. The Emergency Powers (Defence) Act of May 1940 gave Ernest Bevin, Minister of Labour and National Service, complete control over manpower and production and the power to 'direct any person in the United Kingdom to perform such services in the United Kingdom as might be specified'. For example, people could be ordered to move anywhere in the country where the State required them to work.

Many men, liable for conscription to the Forces, were exempted or 'reserved' due to the essential nature of their work, sometimes against their wishes. This system of exemption became more selective from 1941 as increasing numbers of men were required for the Forces. In 1941 when an increase in industrial production became vital, eligible women were conscripted into the services or war work, and other men and women were ordered to register for essential war work and were directed into war industries. The level of control exerted over workers was such that people could be prosecuted for not complying with these directives, or even for absenteeism from essential war work, and such cases did appear in the local newspapers of the time.

"... your life was just organised and dictated to at that time - through the war years. You couldn't do what you wanted. At one time I volunteered for the RAF but the management down there, I don't know, pulled a string or two or something, and I was stopped, you know, it seemed to just go dead. So I wasn't able to proceed with that ... they had what they called 'reserved occupations' at that time, and if you were employed on the type of work say for Rolls Royce then there was no way of getting away from that."
NEW MILL MAN BORN 1920
'RESERVED' WAR WORKER, ENGINEERING

"If you worked at David Brown's that was it! I don't think there were a dozen blokes at Brown's who were called up. There were one or two, yes - but I'm afraid those one or two were those who sort of, er, - fallen out with the management ... we had to sign on and then they decided whether you could stay in engineering or not, depending on what Brown's said."
HUDDERSFIELD MAN BORN 1915
'RESERVED' WAR WORKER, ENGINEERING

"A STRAPPING LAD LIKE YOU OUGHT TO BE AT THE FRONT!"
"THERE'S NO MILK AT THE FRONT, MISSUS!"

Leaving Essential Work Illegally.

Littletown Woman Fined.

"I volunteered for the Air Force ... I'd no need to go in the Air Force, I was on a reserved trade. 'Cause Mr Stringer said to me, 'What are you doing lad? You'll never have to go, I've got you. You know you're covered here'. Because all the other apprentices at Stringer's never went at all. They worked at the ICI and L B Holliday's all through the war, you see they were on restricted - reserved occupations. But I says, 'No, I want to go', I says, 'I've my own life and I prefer to go'. and I did."
HUDDERSFIELD MAN BORN 1921

"We had a lot of people come in from outside industries, such as people who'd been employed in textiles, joinery work. We had quite a heavy recruiting programme and we got some jolly good men in - they were called dilutees at that time because of a union thing."
NEW MILL MAN BORN 1920
'RESERVED' WAR WORKER, ENGINEERING

WORKING FOR WAR

The engineering, chemical and textiles factories and mills of the Kirklees area were vitally important to the national war effort. Firms of all kinds concentrated their production on war supplies from barbed wire to aircraft components. The textile mills wove cloth for uniforms and blankets. Notable local contributions include the production of gears for tanks, aircraft and ships by David Brown's of Huddersfield, and midget submarines (X-craft) made by Thomas Broadbent & Sons Ltd. of Huddersfield. One of these - the X20 'Exemplar' - was one of two midget submarines which played a vital and dangerous role acting as submersible light-ships and guiding the landing craft to the Normandy beaches on D-day.

Unemployment was a thing of the past as men and women worked very long hours making their contribution to winning the war. Factories often worked twenty-four hours a day, seven days a week, even through air raid warnings - each with their team of firewatchers, and aeroplane spotters on the rooftops. Many men and women from this area undertook their war work in other parts of the country.

"You knew also that you were getting inspectors from the War Office to check stuff. This was something totally new and you knew that instead of something being made to do, it had to be right because this was the whole basis of munitions, stuff had to be right or it would be rejected."
HUDDERSFIELD MAN BORN C.1922
WAR WORKER, ENGINEERING

"I was in research all through the war and it was there [David Brown's] where we developed the Merritt-Brown gearbox for tanks. And in fact for a period I used to start work at half-past seven on Monday morning and work all Monday, all Monday night, and then Tuesday morning go home, and then I had to start work again Wednesday morning and work all Wednesday, all Wednesday night and go home Thursday morning and that way. And we did that for a month till we got this gearbox running right, and then you know things eased off then."
HUDDERSFIELD MAN BORN 1915
WAR WORKER, ENGINEERING

"... it started in September the war and I think we went to Tech. till about February and then suddenly we didn't have time for it - the Company said 'Look, you know, we can't allow people to go to Tech., you've got to work overtime'."
NEW MILL MAN BORN 1920
WAR WORKER, ENGINEERING

"... the actual machinery that I was stuck with for quite a while produced big shells in the First War so these were ostensibly shell manufacturing lathes but in actual fact they were altered around a litle bit and used for making tank wheels, the big drive wheels on tanks. And we only roughed the machining out and presumably the parts that we made went elsewhere for finishing off ... Once the war got in full swing we were working seven days a week because of the war effort."
HUDDERSFIELD MAN BORN C.1922
WAR WORKER, ENGINEERING

BY STICKING TO IT, GRIM AND GAY,
WE'VE GOT THE MEASURE OF JERRY!
AND WE'LL SOON HAVE HIM ON THE SPOT
IF WE WORK LIKE HELEN B. MERRY!

A "BAMFORTH" COMIC

"Well we used to come [home from munitions work in Barnoldswick] at Saturday if we couldn't have Friday night off. Then we'd to be back Sunday night you see for Monday morning. It was trolleys [from Milnsbridge] down into Huddersfield and then it was buses from Huddersfield to Bradford. And then from there we went to Skipton and we'd quite a wait then in Skipton. And there was quite a lot of us ... conscripted from all over - not just Huddersfield ... and this bus used to come and pick us all up then to take us [back to Barnoldswick]."
HUDDERSFIELD WOMAN BORN 1908
WAR WORKER, MUNITIONS

WORKING FOR WAR

Work of National Importance.

GROCERY & PROVISIONS.

Owing to the calling up of more branch managers,

THE LION STORES

require

LADY ASSISTANTS to train for responsible positions.
MANAGERS, over 35.
JUNIOR ASSISTANTS, male or female.
UNION WAGES PAID and Good Working Conditions.
Also **INTELLIGENT MAN** for CORN WAREHOUSE
(Protected Establishment).

Apply: J. W. Hillard, Ltd., Serpentine Road,° **Cleckheaton.**

"I started at A V Roe's at Yeadon ... and it meant living over there, either in lodgings or in a hostel for the purpose of housing workers who were uprooted and went to live over there during the emergency period, the war period. And so we [he and his wife] talked it over and decided that I should be better off financially without a doubt, and I wanted to go to - in a twisted way - help the war effort, and get some experience, and it was a bit glamorous to think you were going to build aeroplanes ..."
HUDDERSFIELD MAN BORN 1913
WAR WORKER, ENGINEERING

MIRFIELD WORKERS ENTERTAINED.

◆

E.N.S.A. SHOW IN CANTEEN.

Workers at the Coloured Cotton Spinning Co., Ltd., Mirfield, again enjoyed a non-stop lunch-time concert by E.N.S.A on Tuesday afternoon. The show was given in the firm's canteen—a fine spacious building at Southbrook Mills—one end of which is rigged up with a platform specially for these performances.

Tuesday's bill was an entertaining one, with plenty of comedy and variety in the types of turns. The canteen was packed, and immediately upon finishing lunch the show began and continued non-stop until it was time to return to work again in the factory.

Dick Culley and Joe Hill produced laughs in abundance with their jokes and songs, whilst Miss Mollie Wood

"... Mr A J Riley [Batley] originally, before the war, had been a boiler-maker. And indeed he still made boilers, and air-receivers, for the Admiralty. But we also made engine-bearers for bombers, and we made bombs - but they were smoke bombs, they weren't high explosive. So I was working on this. They were working twenty-four hours a day, seven days a week, where they were twelve-hour shifts on days and on nights. I used to dread and detest the nights which seemed to be endless, particularly in summer when the evenings were long."
BATLEY MAN BORN 1926

"In 1939 I was transferred into the tank gearbox department which produced tanks for the Western desert - for Valentines and Matildas, they produced the gearbox and steering units for those. Then in 1940 I was transferred from Lockwood to Meltham ... there we set up another department in case the department at Lockwood was bombed out, so we could still keep producing. Eventually I transferred again to David Brown's Scar Bottom and there we set up a service department to service tanks that had been used in action. A curious part about that was every Friday we had a party of thirty soldiers came. These were of all ranks from all regiments, the Tank Corps, the Armoured Corps, the Engineers, the Artillery, even Canadians. And they worked with us from Friday to the following Friday and it was quite common to want a lift with something, you just turned round and said 'Give me a lift with this mate'. He may be a Brigadier, he may be a General - they gave you a lift, they worked just like us. We worked with them till the following Friday, they went away and another thirty came."
GOLCAR MAN BORN 1922
WAR WORKER, ENGINEERING

57

"... everybody could smoke. Now previous to the war there was no smoking ... Because girls starting working there and they'd never had girls working there before - in the offices, yes, but girls had to start you know in the works as well - so they allowed smoking then in the works you see, and that had been unheard of previous to that."

HUDDERSFIELD MAN BORN 1915
WAR WORKER, ENGINEERING

"... they had inspectors based on the factory [Brook Motors] from Rolls Royce and we were making parts for the Merlin engine at that time [which] went into the Spitfire ... and certainly the skills that had to be used on those parts were quite different - I mentioned that we were doing more or less a tailor-made job before and we relied on the fitter, but suddenly when this work came along everything had to be spot on and, you know, these people came to instruct us and tell us how precise things had to be and there was no deviation from the tolerances on the drawing. For example in engineering generally if a little mistake's made you can do a little correction or you can sort of do something that'll put things right, but that sort of thing wasn't allowed in the components we were making for Rolls Royce. So suddenly we were changed from a semi-precision shop to a full precision type of engineering."

NEW MILL MAN BORN 1920
WAR WORKER, ENGINEERING

"We also made quite a lot of motors for Russia. Just what those motors were for I don't know but we did quite a lot of work for the Russians during the war down there [Brook Motors]."

NEW MILL MAN BORN 1920
WAR WORKER, ENGINEERING

"When the war started ... we'd all to stop off jobs, whatever we were doing and we'd to tar the windows and the top of the sheds and put some brown paper on when we'd tarred them, and they'd to make them so that there was no light whatsoever. Because if you remember, Lord Haw Haw was saying he'd certainly barrel Huddersfield works. He knew where it was and it wouldn't be long before it was blown up. Well, it made us feel 'We'll have to be careful with these lights'."

ELLAND MAN BORN 1899
WAR WORKER IN HUDDERSFIELD, CHEMICALS

Souvenir Programme of Huddersfield's 'Aid For Russia' Week in February 1942. When Russia entered the war in 1941 local people were asked to work hard to support their new ally with tanks, boots, wool etc. In the illustrated pamphlet the people of Huddersfield gave a pledge to the people of the USSR to '... strive to the utmost of our power to render all aid to your heroic soldiers, sailors and airmen ...'.

"It [production] started to increase before the war, early part of 1939, right from January onwards, people were working seven days a week making things, anything that would contribute - chiefly navy blues for wools, obviously for the Navy, yellows and browns et cetera for mixture for Army, khaki uniforms, this sort of thing. Oh yes, and of course things carried on, all throughout the war they were quite busy."

HUDDERSFIELD MAN BORN 1920
WAR WORKER, CHEMICALS

"We never got bombed but I was on the top of the shop when Sheffield got bombed and we could see all the light in the sky - of course it's only about twenty-eight miles away - and Sheffield got a real hammering you know that night. We could see all the sky lit up and we always thought that they were seeking our place besides Sheffield. Anyway they never found the ICI fortunately and that was it."
ELLAND MAN BORN 1899
WAR WORKER IN HUDDERSFIELD, CHEMICALS

"... they put what we call a shadow factory up, that were the name of it at the time. Now it were to make ammonium nitrates which apparently were a basis for explosive. It's both a fertiliser and it can be made into an explosive, it had two purposes. In fact the Under-Manager told us, he says, 'This is something which can destroy you and it can feed you' - that was actually what he said about it."
HUDDERSFIELD MAN BORN 1904
WAR WORKER, CHEMICALS

"We'd to come every night and they'd show us how to work the fire engine. Every man individually had to stop it and start it and oh they gave us a real training. And we'd some humour in that because we had a bit of fun y'know ... one time they had the hose put in the River Colne and then of course they could get a right good pressure on with those engines. And this chap [had] hold of the hose ... and we put it on at full. It dragged him, and I'll give t'chap his due, he was really game, he stuck to his hose pipe, dragged him all round - wet through to the skin - all round the avenue, and he stuck on. Just gave him a bit of a rough ride on this road and then shut it off. The poor chap was wet through of course ... these silly things went on regularly with the chaps, it broke the monotony of it. But they were very keen were t'ICI, you'd to turn up. Some chaps had worked, y'know they did double shifts and then had to fire-watch - oh y'know 'I'm not coming' - but y'know they fined 'em very heavily."
ELLAND MAN BORN 1899
WAR WORKER IN HUDDERSFIELD, CHEMICALS

"... there was a lot of woman introduced and they did what they could. They pulled their weight did a lot of them, but some of them didn't of course. They weren't really fit for the job but they tried to do their best ... I'd one with me a while but I couldn't say they were great because they couldn't do no lifting and that sort of thing, well you couldn't expect them to do. If it was a heavy job you'd to get a man with you beside a woman. She'd go to t'stores for you, stuff to fetch from the stores and all that sort of thing. But they were fetchers and carriers and sweepers up I should say mainly. But there were a gang come from Barnsley - big strapping girls, and they could swear like men and they could wheel barrows of concrete so they'd been brought up proper in Barnsley, I don't know if they'd been in the pits or not but they were as strong as horses, and they could swear like horses an' all. They were a real tribe. But anyway they were good workers, but our local women they wasn't as good by any means as them lot."
ELLAND MAN BORN 1899
WAR WORKER IN HUDDERSFIELD, CHEMICALS

A Government publication of 1944 which detailed the history of and reasons for the total mobilisation of men and women for the war effort.

WORKING FOR WAR

"... there was one plant in particular - they told us did the then Manager how it kept the firm going and how important the Huddersfield branch was. They were the only firm that made that stuff [Ethylene glycol - used in the cooling system for aero engines and oil] and they worked night and day to put three or four shadow plants in. If they'd have bombed that plant we should have lost the 'Battle of Britain' he said ... Well they called it a shadow plant because ... if a parent plant were bombed they could start up with these ... and they put this stuff in the 'planes and they could go to great heights without it freezing and I'm feared a lot was stolen because it was really right for cleaning soft hats ... and a lot of bottles used to disappear ... It was lovely stuff but it could knock a chap out in no time. It just smelt like pear drops - a lovely smell. In fact you were tempted - 'By, that's grand!' - but it was deadly stuff! In fact I was going up to my works one Monday morning and there were three men staggering. I said 'Well they've been out at t'Black Horse them beggars' they were drunk ... They'd had too much of this here - a sniff of it and it made them drunk, and they were staggering up and down and were holding one another and we thought they'd been to t' Black Horse and gotten drunk, but it wasn't - it made them drunk this Ethylene!"

ELLAND MAN BORN 1899
WAR WORKER IN HUDDERSFIELD,
CHEMICALS

KEEPS WAR WORKERS "FIGHTING FIT"

The Human machine needs ENERGY too

War workers — try Weetabix! Have it at breakfast, take it to the factory or workshop, eat some, some time, every day. You'll find it delicious and — vitally more important — wonderfully sustaining. Weetabix is wheat, the whole of the wheat, with all its valuable mineral salts and vitamins intact. This makes Weetabix so nourishing, so energising, and will make you so much better able to do your war job.

Weetabix
More than a breakfast food

SMALL SIZE 7½D 2 POINTS
LARGE SIZE 1/1D 4 POINTS

Weetabix Ltd., Burton Latimer, Northants.
WX.2.

"... there was a lot of gassing went on, particularly at Aniline plants. I went down [to sick bay] one day, I'd cut my thumb ... and there were a chap there, laid there, and his face was black. I thought 'Oh he's dead'. Anyway I'm just looking at him you know, feeling really sorry and he said 'What time is it lad?' Well, I said 'By God I thought you were dead'. He said 'Don't think nothing about it. I've been cleaning an Aniline tank and I've got gassed' and it turned him all - well, a right deep blue, mind you I was going to say black but I'm exaggerating. I said 'Oh you're bad'. He said 'Oh don't bother, I've had it before'. He said 'When I've gotten owt like, they give me some coffee and then run me up to Nont Sarah's'. And they gave 'em t'rations for the day and they run 'em up and brought them back at night, to sit on the moors while they get it right out of their system. I said 'How long will you be on the sick then?', 'Oh about a fortnight and then I shall be cured'."

ELLAND MAN BORN 1899
WAR WORKER IN HUDDERSFIELD, CHEMICALS

"... another way to send them out when they're getting too much gas in them. They used to set them working on the bowling greens. They must have had twenty helpers on that bowling green. No wonder it won the prize, Yorkshire Merit prize for year after year until they gave up competing. And they'd a foreman, and it used to be t'place where they sent them when they'd had a touch of gas, which lots used to get you know working in it daily. And the doctor would say "We'll get him a job in the fresh air for a while.""

ELLAND MAN BORN 1899
WAR WORKER IN HUDDERSFIELD, CHEMICALS

"... trade began to improve round about 1938, we were doing rather better then. What of course was happening, was that we were re-arming though we didn't quite realise it at the time. But there was more army orders moving about, and khaki serge and RAF serge and Naval serge always had a substantial shoddy content with them, partly from old rags and partly from new cuttings, and there was rather more business to be found when war was declared."

DEWSBURY MAN BORN 1915
WAR WORKER, TEXTILES

"... this was a whole new outfit for a whole new nation that we were suddenly weaving! Everything was full time. I can't remember ever being unemployed and I can't remember anyone around me being unemployed for long. If they got the sack at one place they could get a job at another!"

HUDDERSFIELD WOMAN BORN 1922
WAR WORKER, TEXTILES

WORKING FOR WAR

"The first thing they did when war broke out, they got a load of all t'old weft that they had and got it all wound up and made black-out cloth - got all the place blacked out."
HUDDERSFIELD WOMAN BORN 1926
WAR WORKER, TEXTILES

"... all the windows were totally blacked out and y'see when you were going early in the morning you were going in pitch black, and there were no lights to get home."
HUDDERSFIELD WOMAN BORN 1912
WAR WORKER, TEXTILES

"I went to Aimes at the bottom of Scout Hill and it was at a time when war was looming up you know, and well, most anybody could go and get a job you know, full employment. Those that didn't work didn't want to work and that's how I became to be in textiles."
MIRFIELD MAN BORN 1922
WAR WORKER, TEXTILES

"... other mills such as [Wormald] and Walker's the big blanket mill, they concentrated solely on army blankets and other things I suppose for military use or Government use as we called it, but they made big army blankets. Now then, where I worked it was mostly khaki uniforms, you know soldiers overcoats. We did do a lot of Fire Service AFS uniforms as well but it was more or less khaki heavy stuff."
MIRFIELD MAN BORN 1922
WAR WORKER, TEXTILES

"... the khaki ... ooh it were diabolical stuff. It were all fuzzy and it used to get up your nose and in your eyes and in your hair. And stink! I don't know what it smelt of exactly but I think it must have been treated with something because even when you were out dancing and you danced with a soldier it'd all come off onto your dress. By t'end of an evening you'd have a greeny sheen on whatever you were wearing."
HUDDERSFIELD WOMAN BORN 1926
WAR WORKER, TEXTILES

"We'd what they call a fire-watching team. There were teams of about twenty where I worked, and about I should say every fourth or fifth night, we used to have to go down about ten o'clock and we used to have to sleep in the main office. They provided beds, single beds, and there'd be two men always patrolling the mill with a torch you know, and them two would come back and the next two get out of bed like a roster you know."
MIRFIELD MAN BORN 1922
WAR WORKER, TEXTILES

"I went straight into milling and scouring as I've been all my life and I was only a lad, I wasn't supposed to be in there because I was under age. But as there was an emergency a lot of things were waived off. And I went there just as what they call a bagging lad. And then about 1940 during the Battle of Britain a lot of the older fellers were getting called up and in desperation I suppose they asked me - well they didn't ask me they more or less ordered me that I had to learn to mill which was a - you know, you just couldn't pick it up over night - one of those sort of jobs. And that's how I became to be on the milling side more or less by accident."
MIRFIELD MAN BORN 1922
WAR WORKER, TEXTILES

LIFE GETS WORSE!—BEFORE MY LAD WAS IN THE ARMY HE WORE MY TIES; NOW, THE WIFE'S ON MUNITIONS AND 'SHE'S WEARING MY TROUSERS!

A "BAMFORTH" COMIC

"... [atmosphere] amongst the work people? Well as the war had just broke out a damned good atmosphere to be honest because everybody was together if you understand what I mean. There was no nastiness, no back-biting as we call it, and everybody's mind was focused on one thing you see. Actually I've always said we were a frightened nation because we'd a bachelor war at the time, and I always think that's why everybody stuck together because everybody was frightened and that's what brought everybody together so therefore you'd a terrific atmosphere really. It's an atmosphere that you just couldn't muster up in peace time, no chance."
MIRFIELD MAN BORN 1922
WAR WORKER, TEXTILES

WOMEN AT WORK

The unprecedented conscription of women into the Forces and war work was a logical part of the total planning and direction of the population resource towards the war effort. Eligible women were given an option of the Women's Auxiliary Services (ATS, WRNS or WAAF), Civil Defence, or war industry, and later the Women's Land Army, unless they were already performing work of 'national importance'. Civilian women deemed 'mobile' could be directed out of this area and women were mobilised in from other areas. Other women not eligible for conscription were also registered for war work.

Women filled the places of men conscripted into the Forces from, for example, industry, transport, farming, police and ambulances, taking on and adapting to jobs previously thought of only as 'man's work'. However they rarely received equal pay. Most local women accepted the necessity and importance of war work, and some welcomed the opportunity to work in 'unusual' occupations.

Many women volunteered for the services and war work before conscription, and many not eligible for conscription also undertook war work, including much voluntary service. In addition to their normal working hours, eligible women were also liable, like men, for compulsory Civil Defence and fire-watching duties. Many working women also of course had domestic responsibilities with children to look after, shopping to do and the home to run.

"Girls were drafted into places like Brook Motors and David Brown's and that, and doing night shifts y'know. They got very weary and run down, very tired a lot of them did, cause it was heavy work a lot of it ... A friend of mine she'd a real battle with the authorities because she'd her old mother, and they were saying well, she wasn't married, she'd no ties, they were going to send her out of town, y'know, out of Huddersfield. But she battled on and stuck to her guns and she stayed in Huddersfield - I think she went to ICI."
HUDDERSFIELD WOMAN BORN 1915

THUMBS UP, EVERYBODY, WE'LL SEE IT THROUGH!

"... when war broke out in 1939 I was working [in a mill office]. My husband was called up in 1940 and the Head Clerk was called up around the same time and I took his job. I was Head Clerk during the war ... there was a lot more women came into the mill then because, you know, some of the men were called up. I did want to go into the WAAFs but I was considered to have a reserved job - why they took the Head Clerk, the man, I don't know!"
MARSDEN WOMAN BORN 1914

"... it [war] brought a lot more work and all the women went out to work then, but previous to that of course married women rarely went out although some in textiles did. It's always been tradition in textiles hasn't it for married women to work as well."
HUDDERSFIELD WOMAN BORN 1923

"My wife was detailed to come into what they called munitions. Originally she'd worked in a jeweller's shop, but she came into Brook's on the instruction of the authorities - you know that was quite common, you know, shop girls."
NEW MILL MAN BORN 1920

"He [husband] were called up into t'Air Force and so then of course I were on me own, we had no children, and so I went into t'ARP and did a bit in t'ARP, then I went onto t'ambulances and from t'ambulances I went into t'Police Force."
LIVERSEDGE WOMAN BORN 1910

WOMEN AT WORK

SATURDAY, JULY 19, 1941.

"IT'S A GRAND JOB!"

Says Batley's Woman Porter

"I felt I must do my bit like the rest of them," says Mrs. Gertrude Dawson, Belvedere Road, Mount Pleasant, Batley, who is the first woman porter in the district. She is 48 years of age.

"... you'd to do a special war job or go in the Forces, and so I went to work first of all as a goods porter on the railway. Now there was about three shifts and one started at midnight, Sunday night. The rest of the week it was ten, but Sunday night it was midnight. It was terrible in the dark winter, having to go get ready when everybody was going to bed, to go to work. And I remember this particular winter was cold because I put two of everything on and you know I was fairly plump to start with, so it didn't do anything for how I looked. But of course there was nobody to see you, and it was pitch dark, it was in the black-out of course."
HUDDERSFIELD WOMAN BORN 1920
PORTER, HUDDERSFIELD STATION

"... we had some very heavy wagons to unload, and in the winter the big sheets were covered in snow - we had to remove these before you could get at the goods. And if it was iron bars, well it was terribly hard ... Another wagon which we hated to do was the tripe wagon, you could smell it a mile off - undressed tripe smells terrible - we would put scarves round our noses so we couldn't smell this tripe ... that was a fairly hard job, it was the shift work really that was the worst, specially in the black-out."
HUDDERSFIELD WOMAN BORN 1920
PORTER, HUDDERSFIELD STATION

"I desperately wanted to join up but y'see good workers they wanted to keep you, so with these Government contracts they got you out of it."
HUDDERSFIELD WOMAN BORN 1926
WAR WORKER, TEXTILES

"I didn't want to go into munitions and I didn't want to go doing farm work. [My husband] was brought up on a smallholding and his mum said 'Don't go, it's horrible in winter', so I went into the Army."
HUDDERSFIELD WOMAN BORN 1920
ATS

"I was reserved for about two years. Normally you had to go at eighteen but because I worked at David Brown's and at that time I was in the Planning Office, I was considered to be in a reserved occupation. But later on I suppose they got short of manpower, they started calling more people up and I was called up then. I had to go for an interview initially in Meltham, and I was asked if I wanted to go in the services or if I wanted to go on munitions. And if I had wanted to go on munitions I would have had to go to a place in Lancashire, Barnoldswick that's it, where there was a munition works. I actually opted to join the WAAF, the Air Force, and then later on I got a letter saying there was no vacancies at the moment in the Air Force, would I like to join the Wrens so I did."
HUDDERSFIELD WOMAN BORN 1923
WREN

ATTENTION!

THE WOMEN'S SALUTE
The great part women have played in the War has yet to be told. When it is, it will be a great story
—of their important place in the Forces.
—of their heroic work in the hospitals
—of their devoted work in the many voluntary services
—and not the least, in the splendid efforts for War Savings,

WOMEN OF MIRFIELD!
Crown your efforts this week by helping to reach that

£70,000 Target.

Invest every penny you can in: 3% Savings Bonds 1960-70; 2½% National War Bonds 1952-54; 3% Defence Bonds. Savings Certificates. Savings Stamps. The Post Office Savings Bank.

MIRFIELD SALUTE the SOLDIER WEEK
MAY 13-20.

"I didn't fancy going in the Forces and ... they called me up for an interview and I could, you know, choose and I put down for munitions at home if I could go. You see there was Brown's and places like that but I had to go away ... They made - it was the Rover company - made aeroplane engines ... And in this factory there was a petrol tank where they used to use it for cleaning all their parts. I was an Inspector, and I hadn't been in long when I developed a right bad rash. Course it was a big place and they had their own doctor, and I had to go and see him and as soon as he saw me he said, 'Out of the factory', he said, 'You have got paraffin rash.' I said, 'Well I don't touch any paraffin.' ... it is what I was inhaling, and it had got into my blood stream ... So I went into the stores at the same factory which was more like shop work then ... I felt all the time I'd have been much better at home, you know, I felt as though I was wasting my time and theirs. I thought they could have carried on, those men in that stores, and I would have been better at home doing another job."

HUDDERSFIELD WOMAN BORN 1908
WAR WORKER, MUNITIONS, BARNOLDSWICK

"It [lodgings] was an attic bedroom and it was a double bed and when I went to work on the morning another girl went into the bed that had been working nights. Yes that is quite true! So the bed was warm when she went to bed wasn't it? Would have cooled off a bit before I went to bed wouldn't it! Yes, but apart from that it was good lodgings, she looked after us very well."

HUDDERSFIELD WOMAN 1908
WAR WORKER, MUNITIONS, BARNOLDSWICK

"MISS BROWN! YOU'RE NOT TURNING YOUR SHELLS OUT PROPERLY!"
"WELL, WHAT D'YER THINK I AM---A BLINKING HEN?"

ARMAMENT FACTORY
SHELL DEPT

BOROUGH OF BATLEY.

WAR-TIME NURSERY, "MAYVILLE,"
DARK LANE, BATLEY.

There are at present TEN VACANCIES at the above Nursery for CHILDREN from 0—5 years. Parents must be engaged directly or indirectly on War Work.
Applications should be sent to the Matron or the undersigned.
WM. J. FRAIN,
Medical Officer of Health.
Medical Officer's Department,
Market Place, Batley.   514

"The Government put on childrens nursery schools and my daughter went at eleven months old - she could talk and walk at that age, she was quite forward. And there were probation nurses. And we used to pay five shillings a week if we wanted to help the war - soldiers, airmen, sailors wives had priority. So for five shillings a week I used to take her at eight o'clock for me to get to work, and pick her up at four or five y'see, and they were fed and looked after ..."

BIRSTALL WOMAN BORN 1917

"... you'd to work shifts for a lot of time 'cause most places worked twenty-four hours a day you know, weaving khaki and that for t'Forces and - oh, I used to hate going half-past eleven while half-past seven or half-past eight, and my boyfriend, he'd be working until eight o'clock and we'd meet each other and then it'd be time to say goodbye, you know, it were awful. And then if you'd to start at seven o'clock on a morning and you couldn't get a bus, you'd to walk right up to Birkby's - it were awful. And we used to have fog in those days. I've seen me walk home in thick fog at half-past seven at night - it's taken us an hour and a half to get home, wondering where you were and black-out as well. You didn't know where you were!"

HECKMONDWIKE WOMAN BORN 1926
WAR WORKER, TEXTILES

WOMEN AT WORK

It was a whole new way of working for those women coming into the engineering factories and onto the 'shop floor'. Here two local women tell something of their experiences at David Brown's.

"I wove till t'war, 1942, and then I'd to go to work at Brown's. Although, actually I were weaving khaki shirting at Shaw's [S H Shaw's] but through t'labour they called us up y'see. Well my husband was in t'Middle East so they couldn't really send me away, but they had to go doing a wartime job, so they sent me up to Brown's. And I allus remember one of t'women said 'And what are these I'm making?' y'see, thinking she were building a tank. And they said 'Oh, them's gears for bacon machines', and she were disgusted - been weaving, actually weaving khaki shirting and you're put on there! But that were t'way they were during t'war, you had to go where you were sent.

"I had [enjoyed it] at Brown's. I mean you knew you had to work but there was a bit of variety. Y'see being such a big place there were allus somebody acting the fool somehow or other, and they'd got dances on a night shift. Y'see you had an hour for your dinner at twelve o'clock so it got a bit boring, and they started letting women ... go up and dance [in the canteen] and then it gradually got while t'fellers were coming up - Oh we got to having gala nights on a Friday night before t'end of t'war - Oh it were fun.

"We worked nights and days, twelve hours each. First three nights you were on after you'd been on days, ooh it were hard work. When it got about three o'clock you were nearly asleep stood up, but you got used to it ...

"[I] started in January '42 while about January '46. They gradually kicked us out like when t'fellers started coming back, y'know, from the war."
KIRKBURTON WOMAN BORN 1918
WAR WORKER, ENGINEERING

WE'LL PEG ALONG ALL RIGHT
NOW RE-ARMAMENT'S IN FULL SWING,
SO WORK LIKE HELEN B. MERRY---
OPTIMISM'S THE THING!

"... they'd just started employing girls on inspection and so my eldest sister and I were the first to go in. They used to whistle when we walked down the bays and we used to go in two's at first, and then gradually they got more girls in so it wasn't too bad.

"... all the floors were oily and they'd all bits of metal stuck in so that you got them stuck on your shoes, you know, as you walked through. You used to pass all the big turning machines, first of all big lathes, and all oil and noise and it always had a smell, and your clothes always seemed to smell of it. And of course I hadn't worked where men were before - we'd sort of worked all women together more or less, and that seemed strange.

"... we'd to wear an overall ... but we didn't fancy them and so we bought our own and we used to have to scrub them down in the cellar at weekends to get them clean, and then we had to have these nasty little caps.

WOMEN AT WORK

"... there were cages built in the centre of the machine shop, and we worked inside this cage if you were on inspection, and you'd benches all round and they taught us how to use a micrometer and how to read a blue print.

"There were bevels and spur gears ... and then some would have a bore ... then you had templates which you had to put inside and feel if the 'feel' was just right. Well, when they were turned and polished it wasn't too bad but when they were in the rough state, oh, they were oily and terrible and so I used to go to the Foreman and say 'I can't handle these they're cutting all my hands to bits' so I said 'Can I have some gloves for picking these nasty ones up' and he used to say as soon as he saw us going 'You can't have any more gloves'.

"... they had a little etching machine and you had to etch numbers on gears for Aircraft ... And they found out I was quite a good printer. So I got this job sitting down, and I didn't mind that although it was a bit hot and all the sparks used to fly as you were etching the numbers on.

"... we had to work Saturdays, and we had to work overtime until half-past seven, and really at the height of - I don't know, think it'd be the height of the Battle of Britain - we'd to work Sundays as well. And that year we didn't have a holiday - we'd to work all through, so it was dark and they painted all the roof so that we didn't have any sunlight in at all, all the time and oh they were long days, they were terrible sometimes. Sometimes it wasn't bad but on these long days it used to be dreadful! And you came out and it was dark you see, and then in summer you came out into the sunlight.

LET THEM HAVE THEIR LIPSTICK,
BLESS THEIR LITTLE HEARTS;
SURELY THEY HAVE PROVED THEMSELVES
GIRLS OF MANY PARTS!

A "BAMFORTH" COMIC

"Towards the end of the war they fixed a room up with a lamp and you sort of stripped off to the waist and put a halter top on and went under this sunlamp because they thought we hadn't been getting enough sunlight. So at least that, when I think back, that was something.

"There was a bit of class distinction I didn't like. When we were on inspection then it said 'Females' on our toilets, and the one in the office said 'Ladies' and it used to really annoy me this - why one said 'Females' and the other said 'Ladies'!

"I'd have hated to have done that job I suppose, but I don't think you questioned it. The point was we had all to do something and that was it! I know when the war finished you wanted to get out as quickly as you could. You couldn't say that you enjoyed working there, you didn't, because it was dirty. But we did have - there was comradeship and laughs - and we did have fun I suppose at times. But it got very boring if you'd a whole stack of things to do. They were all alike, and you were just sort of testing them all the time and the days seemed endless."

HUDDERSFIELD WOMAN BORN 1922
WAR WORKER, ENGINEERING

WOMEN'S LAND ARMY

As farms lost men to the Forces and factories, thousands of women who became known as 'Land girls' took their places. Some volunteered, others were conscripted, opting for land work rather than munitions or the Forces. Some became part of mobile teams despatched by War Agricultural Committees as, when and where their services were required. Others could find themselves alone on a small farm away from official surveillance or companionship. The women undertook a wide variety of work, often extremely heavy and involving long hours. For many it was their first time away from home, and it changed their lives.

"... they [farmers] kept saying 'I don't think you will be strong enough to do it' you see, because you know it's different from working inside sewing, and then going out and doing a lot of heavy lifting and that you know. But anyway I think I managed to do it all right."
HUDDERSFIELD WOMAN BORN 1919
LAND GIRL

"I must have been about eighteen when I went into the Land Army and then my life changed considerably. I don't think you ever go back into the same pattern once you leave home ... I went into the Land Army in Devon, but I was snatched away from home - you had no option."
HUDDERSFIELD WOMAN BORN 1922
LAND GIRL

"My paternal grandfather was a farmer ... whether it was a kind of throwback to that I don't know. I just wanted to go into the Land Army. Me father was totally against me joining up at all and me mother said it would do me good."
HUDDERSFIELD WOMAN BORN 1925
LAND GIRL

"I went to Leeds to the Land Army centre there and picked up my uniform ... You had to give your own coupons in the Land Army because we were never considered part of the Forces, it was separate. So we never got regular leaves. If the farmer could spare you he'd let you go for a week if you were at a good place. If not, you'd a struggle - your Land Army Representative really had to fight for you to get you time off ... We weren't getting paid like the other Forces were because each individual farmer paid what he thought. If you had an injustice this is when you went to your Land Army Representative."
HUDDERSFIELD WOMAN BORN 1925
LAND GIRL

"I was posted to a general farm ... I did a week about there and then I was really fed up, so instead of going to see the Land Army Representative which I should have done, I packed me belongings and I hitch-hiked home ... they told my mother at Leeds that they'd had so many complaints about him that he would never get another Land girl."
HUDDERSFIELD WOMAN BORN 1925
LAND GIRL

I'M SURE SOME O' THEM GALS HAVE GOT A WIDER UNDERSTANDING SINCE THEY CAME HERE!

"I did a months training at East Sussex School of Agriculture where we learnt either to milk or tractor drive or horticulture or just general farm work. Well, I'd never seen a cow in me life but they said 'Oh you'll be a milker'- you never really had any choice. So after a struggle they got me sat down behind a cow - there were no machines then of course so it was all hand milking ... before the month's up you're a fully fledged milker."
HUDDERSFIELD WOMAN BORN 1923
LAND GIRL

"I went to a place called Caistor in Lincolnshire and I was supposed to take up a position that was going to be vacated by another Land girl and she was going to marry an American, but after about a couple of weeks the American jilted her so she stayed. And I was able to work there for a while but there wasn't another place for me ... That was doing pest destruction and that was where we went out with the snares and the traps and the poison and did quite a lot of rabbit and rat catching in that area."
HUDDERSFIELD WOMAN BORN 1925
LAND GIRL

"I went back on to what we called 'the gang' which was a crowd of girls employed by the Agriculture Committee, Kent Agriculture Committee, and we went out doing threshing, strawberry picking, apple picking, cherry picking - any job that was in season at the time. And in between those jobs if anybody wanted a milker I had to go and do two or three weeks on a dairy farm which broke the monotony, especially when it was potato picking time, 'cause we hated potato picking!"
HUDDERSFIELD WOMAN BORN 1923
LAND GIRL

"I was a dairy maid most of the time, and then delivering milk, and then odd jobs ... sometimes the cows gave more milk at certain times of the year, but we weren't supposed to let people have more than their ration - but we did! Well he got into trouble once did our farmer ... and he had to go to court and I had to go to court as well, I remember that, as a witness."
HUDDERSFIELD WOMAN BORN 1919
LAND GIRL

Women's Land Army in Suffolk.

'Possibly initially they [farmers] may have thought 'What are they going to be like?' but the girls really turned out to be marvellous y'know ... I can remember once I was on the farm one weekend, there was a delivery of grain ... and this driver wouldn't unload the grain and so he sat by while I got 70 cwt. of grain off that lorry by myself ... It took me a good while, but I could do it then, pull the sack onto me back ... Oh I'm lying - he didn't sit by - he got on the wagon and he pushed the sacks to the side onto my back."
HUDDERSFIELD WOMAN BORN 1925
LAND GIRL

"I didn't like getting up early very much, but I mean it wasn't because of the work. I used to enjoy going onto the farm and doing the work ... I liked being there but I was homesick."
HUDDERSFIELD WOMAN BORN 1925
LAND GIRL

"We just didn't think there was going to be an end to that life because we were just happy plodding along as we were. We didn't care how hard the work was really - we just liked it."
HUDDERSFIELD WOMAN BORN 1923
LAND GIRL

'BEVIN BOYS'

In 1941 as it became clear that Britain was suffering a severe shortfall in coal production due to labour shortages in the mines, an Essential Works Order was placed which forced miners to stay in their jobs. Many miners who had been called up to the Forces were released and sent back to the mines, and former miners working elsewhere were traced and compelled to re-enter the mines. However there was still a shortage, and from December 1943 Ernest Bevin, Minister of Labour, directed one in ten of all young men conscripted for National Service down the mines, a measure which was generally very unpopular with those selected. They became known as 'Bevin Boys'. One such local conscript tells his story here

"I was so keen [to join the RAF] and when it came time for me to go for my medical ... I went in fear and trembling that I wouldn't pass the medical because it was a very strict and stringent one for the air crew ... in the event I passed A1 and I came back on cloud nine. But by this time I was working on war work and I was a turner in a factory which made, amongst other things, bombs would you believe and because of this it was work of national importance. Quite a number of people had been leaving and it had been decided that people should not be allowed to be called up if it was deemed that they were doing work of national importance.

"I was informed when I got back to work that I had been placed on the reserve list, without consulting me. I was absolutely furious. I remember dashing upstairs to see the Manager but of course it didn't get me anywhere and that was it. And so I had to make the best of it. I was bitterly disappointed.

"After a month or two of being in this situation, one morning through the letterbox came an official looking letter ... this official looking document told me - I was informed that it was a ballot, it was all done on ballot - I had been drawn out of the ballot and therefore would I present myself to Askern Training Centre near Doncaster.

"To say that I was absolutely horrified would be to understate it. I always thought whilst I was working in engineering that there was a possibility of getting out, but I thought that once I'd been re-directed down the mine there would be very litle chance. But although I wouldn't have admitted it to anyone at the time, the real reason why I was horrified about the possibility of going down mines was the thought that I may be claustrophobic, that I may lose my nerve and run to the bottom of the pit shaft yelling 'Let me out'. And so I tried, I took this calling up notice for the mines, I took it to work with me and I remember going up the stairs into the Manager's Office and slamming it on his desk and saying 'Look, a couple of months ago you reserved me against my will from the Forces. Now this has come and I'm called up into the mines.' I said 'Now look, this is your responsibility, for God's sake get me out of this'.'Oh don't worry lad, we'll see to it. It'll be all right, forget about it' But of course it wasn't all right.

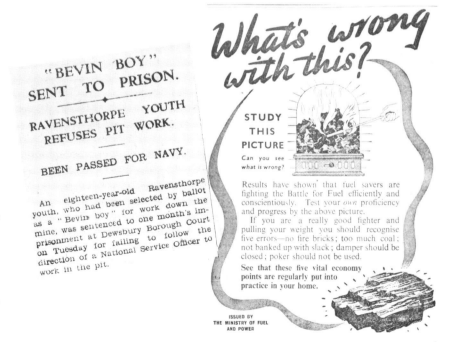

"BEVIN BOY" SENT TO PRISON.

RAVENSTHORPE YOUTH REFUSES PIT WORK.

BEEN PASSED FOR NAVY.

An eighteen-year-old Ravensthorpe youth, who had been selected by ballot as a "Bevin boy" for work down the mine, was sentenced to one month's imprisonment at Dewsbury Borough Court on Tuesday for failing to follow the direction of a National Service Officer to work in the pit.

What's wrong with this?

STUDY THIS PICTURE

Can you see what is wrong?

Results have shown that fuel savers are fighting the Battle for Fuel efficiently and conscientiously. Test your *own* proficiency and progress by the above picture.

If you are a really good fighter and pulling your weight you should recognise five errors—no fire bricks; too much coal; not banked up with slack; damper should be closed; poker should not be used.

See that these five vital economy points are regularly put into practice in your home.

ISSUED BY
THE MINISTRY OF FUEL
AND POWER

'BEVIN BOYS'

"When we first started as Bevin Boys we were not taken seriously at all. We found that the miners were a very, very closed community. They looked upon us as rather soft and we didn't know what it was all about, and we weren't taken seriously as I say. But gradually some of us proved ourselves and eventually we went on to be trained in all manner of work.

"The mine at which I worked in South Yorkshire, Barnborough, was a sort of show place ... all the latest in mining technology ... seams of coal six foot thick ... I was allowed to leave South Yorkshire and come to live at home and to work at Nutter Lane Pit. Hah, yes! Well this was really something else. At first, my first few weeks, I have never been so utterly, completely bone-weary. I have never ached so much, I have never been in such despair in all my life ... The only mechanisation they had was an electric winding engine which dropped us down the shaft ... and the coal seams were very shallow. One would be fortunate to have a twenty-two inch roof height ... they looked for all the world like a whole series of - not much bigger than rabbit burrows. My first day I could not believe that people could actually go down them ... the man who was detailed to take me in suddenly said, 'You go up there', and immediately twisted his tub round at right angles, and disappeared up one of these little rabbit holes. I wouldn't have believed it possible, but he did, and he disappeared ... There were great sharp pieces of rock projecting from the sides, and from the roof. I've still got marks on my back, as a result of this - they lacerated one's back, in an unwary moment.

"Shall we say looking back that it was an experience and as such I wouldn't have missed it. But no way, I would not send my worst enemy to work under such conditions as were in force at Nutter Lane Pit! I really could not believe that such primitive conditions could exist in the 1940s."
BATLEY MAN BORN 1926
BEVIN BOY

A Huddersfield Bevin Boy photographed in 1944 outside his home in Lockwood, on his way to work at Emley Moor Colliery. There were no pit baths at the time so he had to leave and return home wearing his pit clothing. This man enjoyed his time as a Bevin Boy, and though he could have left in 1947, he opted to stay in for a further two years.

WARTIME FOR CHILDREN

Children during the war years suddenly found the whole pattern of their lives disrupted. Their family might be separated and they were affected by rationing, shortages, the black-out, and all other aspects of wartime life. Air raids and air raid precautions interrupted their lessons and their sleep. Those who were children at that time however, mostly say that for them war was an adventure - exciting rather than frightening. And there were some aspects of wartime life that were positively welcomed!

"If the siren - the 'All Clear' - didn't go before early morning, two o'clock, we didn't have to go to school until ten o'clock. If it went after two o'clock we had the morning off, and therefore we'd only to go to school in the afternoon. So we were all thinking, 'Oh I hope it lasts a bit longer, oh don't go', you know, 'don't go - don't go just yet,' you know, because that meant we could have the whole morning off school."
DEWSBURY WOMAN BORN 1930

"The main thing I can remember about classes during the war was having to have fitted first of all for gas masks, which was quite an event because we didn't do lessons and everybody had to have a different fitting, and so therefore it took a nice long time an' we were all comparing these new things, you see, and how funny it felt. Then after that we had to have a practice every day, about ten minutes or so, you know, doing lessons with these gas masks on. Which there again was, you know, a novelty."
DEWSBURY WOMAN BORN 1930

Huddersfield schoolchildren doing PE lessons wearing gas masks. There was frequent practice of putting on and wearing gas masks at school in order to get the children used to them.

WARTIME FOR CHILDREN

"... the year the war started, the summer, we had an extended holiday of about three, four weeks because the air raid shelter wasn't ready, so we couldn't go to school as a group ..."
DEWSBURY WOMAN BORN 1930

"... before we had a proper brick air raid shelter built near the school we had to use a tunnel which went from the Combs Pit to the Ings Pit. There were two collieries owned by Inghams, it was before mines were nationalised, and they had a tunnel which ran between the two pits, through the hills - right through the hill in Thornhill from one side - from one pit to the other, and we used to have to go down from the school for an air raid practice and we'd go to the tunnel. They would stop the tubs running and then we would go into that tunnel and that was our air raid shelter in the early years of the war."
MIRFIELD MAN BORN 1930

LET 'EM ALL COME!

BASEMENT

"Well they decided we weren't going to go to school full-time, we just went part-time, I think we went mornings some weeks and afternoons other weeks, because they called the teachers up. And if you were married you didn't teach, you know, if you were a lady you didn't teach. So they brought all the retired men back and all the married ladies because all the young men went to war. So immediately we just went part-time to school which we thought were great you know."
HECKMONDWIKE WOMAN BORN 1926

"I remember when they [gas masks] were first issued at school, some very rude raspberry noises were made ... one had to breath out quite strongly in order to force out the air, whereupon it gave out a rather rude raspberry kind of noise. And of course we children were delighted in blowing these raspberries all over class!"
BATLEY MAN BORN 1926

I SHAN'T NEED TELLING WHAT TO DO, WHEN ONE DAY OUR DREAMS COME TRUE!

"I always remember we thought we'd try to deceive the teacher because, y'know, you couldn't eat sweets you see. Any sweets had to be for playtime and that was it. And I remember going to a shop in Boothroyd Lane and buying some tiny sweets, and thinking 'Oh, when we have gas mask drill this morning we shall be able to, y'know, eat sweets while we have gas masks on'. But it didn't quite work out for although they were only tiny, the restricted movement that you had, y'know, it made that ten minutes seem an awful long time. And we were thinking we were doing something that we shouldn't do, you see - eating in class and teacher wouldn't know. But as I say we were really relieved to take t'gasmasks off because they were sort of scenty - little scenty gum things. Only small, but with the enclosed space of the gasmask, made it all a little bit too much and ten minutes seemed an awful long time."
DEWSBURY WOMAN BORN 1930

WARTIME FOR CHILDREN

Without doubt the war dominated the lives of local children. They followed the progress of the war avidly, knew where the troops were at any one time, and could easily identify, model or draw aircraft or ships. Although traditional games continued to be played, reminiscences clearly reveal the wartime influences over play. And of course a topic always near to any childs heart was the availability or lack of sweets.

"If the teacher had have said 'I want you to draw a Spitfire today', the kids themselves would have been very much up in arms if anybody had drawn anything that didn't look like a Spitfire ... And also, most of the lads used to be whittling away at pieces of wood - something that you never see now - and the same thing would apply. If the teacher said, 'I want you to make a wooden Blenheim', well - you would expect it to look like a Blenheim and not like a Wellington. I think, as with most of the lads in my class, we could have certainly recognised any aircraft or any ship given a silhouette, because it was just part of life."
HUDDERSFIELD MAN BORN 1931

Local schoolchildren training in the use of a stirrup pump.

"... as we went to school we used to buy a carrot not sweets, or a bag of, I think it was oats, a small bag of oats."
CLECKHEATON WOMAN BORN 1932

"My father used to send Turkish delight and sugared almonds and things like this from Egypt ... so we were quite well off compared with a lot of people."
HUDDERSFIELD MAN BORN 1931

"... there was a [Home Guard] practice area at the side of Gomersal cricket field, where they hung up straw bags, where they did their bayonet practice there - and we did it as well ... we just used a stick."
GOMERSAL MAN BORN 1928

"There was some army gun emplacements at the top and we used to go up there and play. There was a little quarry, and the soldiers sometimes used to practise with live ammunition ... we used to virtually sit by the side of them while they were having target practice and then after they'd finished and all marched off we'd go scrambling in among the rocks collecting the spent cartridges and spent bullets - we had quite a big collection at one time."
HUDDERSFIELD MAN BORN 1931

"After those bombs landed on the barley fields [in Gomersal] we had quite a good collection of shrapnel ... it had some prize because it had the German eagle and writing on it y'know. That was a prize bit, not just a piece of metal."
GOMERSAL MAN BORN 1928

"We treat it seriously among some of the kids - what to do in case the Germans did land. Y'know how we would go around puncturing their bikes and things like this and how you could tell if it was a German by offering him some fish and chips and then seeing if he asked for vinegar or whether he pronounced it correctly [or said 'winegar']. There was all sorts, and it sounds ludicrous, and yet I can remember as kids we treat all this very seriously. Y'know, how we would stop the German advance by a lot of these different tricks, although a lot of them I suppose we got from the comics because this sort of thing was in the comics."
HUDDERSFIELD MAN BORN 1931

EVACUEES

Although nearby towns such as Leeds and Bradford were included in the Government scheme to evacuate children and mothers from high risk areas to safer areas, the children of Kirklees were not evacuated during the war. Instead Kirklees was a 'reception' area and people throughout the district opened up their homes to children and families escaping from the bombing of cities such as London and Hull. Hundreds of evacuees arrived in Batley in 1941. One of those evacuees who came from Hull has happy memories of his three year stay in the town.

"... the nearest bomb [in Hull] was about, oh, eighty yards away, and it fell in a timber yard, because we lived quite close to the docks, and all the houses in our street lost their roofs, the windows, window frames and everything, but the walls themselves didn't come down. There was lots of plaster came down, and in fact we were hit you know with big chunks of plaster coming off the walls, and I was actually hit with a brick on my back, but nobody was seriously hurt.

"... evacuation was an option that people could have before bombs had even started to fall, and my mother just wouldn't hear of it. But after we'd been bombed out of the first house ... the centre of the city was still being bombed and the dock was being bombed badly ... then a lot of bombs fell locally in the area we were living in. Now nothing hit us, not even remotely, but we heard a full stick of bombs exploding coming nearer and nearer ... very, very dramatic and I think that made up my mother's mind. She just said, you know, words to the effect 'To hell with this, we've had enough, we're going' and that's how we became evacuated. Just reported to the Town Hall and said we want to go, pack a suitcase, report at the railway station and that was it.

"... everybody with a cardboard box with a gas mask in, plus whatever luggage they'd got in the way of shopping bags or suitcases - and a luggage label tied to your coat. A lot of them were going - the children were going - with no parents, and I think that's how most people went, but in our case we went as a family.

"... they'd asked for volunteers in the area to take various people. Now in our case the people who we eventually went to in Batley, they'd offered to take a mother and child, So they were expecting when they opened the door to find a young woman and a baby, instead of which they opened the door and found a young woman, baby and two sons. Now they'd only got one bedroom at their disposal so the whole four of us had to share the one room, so no, there wasn't much choice - people were just allocated.

"I think the first impression was the impression of the hills. Where we'd lived in Hull was absolutely flat ... it was the first hilly place we'd ever been to, and even to see things like quarries! Again, it seemed a very bustling sort of place, which may sound strange having come from a sea port where there was always plenty of activity. I mean as lads we used to play on the docks so there was plenty of work going on, but when we came to Batley there always seemed to be plenty of people going to work or from work, you know shift work, and the miners going to Shaw Cross Colliery. There was also the big change - I think it's the first time we'd ever seen clogs so as lads we wanted a pair of clogs with clog irons on - that seemed very attractive - it was part of the uniform to join in!

CIVIL DEFENCE

EVACUATION WHY AND HOW?

PUBLIC INFORMATION LEAFLET NO. 3

Read this and keep it carefully. You may need it.

Issued from the Lord Privy Seal's Office July, 1939.

Government Information Leaflet 'Evacuation Why and How?' which gave local people information about the scheme. Kirklees was a 'reception' area taking in evacuees from more dangerous areas of the country.

EVACUEES

"Times like winter, when there was snow on the ground - we had a home-made sledge and we could sledge all the way down from the top of Caulms Wood down to Commonside, and down to Upper Soothill. You know, total run must be getting on for a mile. There was no hill at all in Hull, - I suppose in a way it was like being sent to Switzerland - you know, to finish your schooling off, almost - so there was lots of different things that we'd not come across.

GOSH, MISTER! ARE YOU EVACUATING THE TOWN?

A "BAMFORTH" COMIC

BATLEY WELCOMES THE CHILDREN.

WARM RECEPTION OF EVACUEES.

LONDON OFFICIAL'S HIGH PRAISE.

KIDDIES LOVE THE FARMS.

Batley is, and very rightly should be, a happier place this week. And for one of the best reasons. It has taken into its midst and away from the danger of the flying bomb, 500 children from London.

Many of these children, ranging in age from 5 to 14 years, appeared heavy-eyed, blanched and weary from their recent experiences of long spells spent in shelters, but the warmth of the welcome they received from the townspeople here, refreshing sleep, undisturbed in comfortable beds and all the efforts of their new "foster parents" to make them comfortable and contented worked wonders. A sparkle returned to their eyes, tears which had been evoked by their departure from home were replaced by a smile, the rosy bloom of healthy childhood returned to drive the pallor from their cheeks. In short they soon became once again bright carefree children playing games and showing high spirits Surely indeed, Batley is a happier place.

Batley people have welcomed these children with the warmth of hearts, and though that is perhaps only what

"The people themselves, you know the local neighbours and that, seemed very friendly but for the first week or two at school it was a bit traumatic because we were two complete strangers who may as well have landed off the moon, and the number of fights we got into was dreadful really. But once we'd got over that there seemed to be plenty going on.

"Also, I mean, I wouldn't give the impression we were not made welcome, even at school, because the very first Saturday I was there I remember a group of strange lads appearing at our door and asking my mother if we could go to the cinema with them. They were going down into Batley to the cinema ... and we all set off from Bromley Street to go to Batley station and then from there to the town centre and that was my very first weekend in Batley. And the footpath ran along the top of the railway cutting and I fell off. So I fell down the quarry and was knocked out before we even got to the cinema!

"In our case things worked out very well, you know, we were made very welcome and we lived with these people for almost a year and then what happened the - I would imagine it was the officials in Batley at the Town Hall following a request from my mother - they got us a house of our own.

"It was an adventure really. I don't know if it would have been any different if my mother hadn't have been with us. You see, I wasn't having to write home to my mother. I was writing to my father, but my father was away in any case, so even if I'd have been in Hull I'd have still have been doing that. Batley was an adventurous place to live.

"I think my mother was missing relatives and close friends. And, at that time things were getting quieter, you know [in Hull] ... But it was a bit ironic when we moved back, that's when the flying bombs started coming ... I can remember a flying bomb falling one night in front of our local cinema, just as the people were all leaving, and some lads in my class - I mean personal friends - they were killed."

HUDDERSFIELD MAN BORN 1931.
EVACUEE FROM HULL TO BATLEY

EVACUEES

Many evacuated children arrived without their mothers to look after them. Stories of a 'cattle market' system of hosts choosing their evacuees are commonplace. The national evacuation scheme highlighted social and economic differences in the country - both evacuees and hosts discovered worlds and living conditions they did not know existed. In some cases evacuation caused friction and frustration, and in others it forged bonds for life. Other 'strangers' in the area who lived with Kirklees families included refugees from the occupied Channel Islands, munitions workers, soldiers evacuated from Dunkirk, and soldiers actually billeted in the locality.

"We had one [evacuee from London] a little girl - Pamela ... they asked certain people if they'd have these kids. Some, you know, said yes they would - fair enough, you went to pick them up at the station. But these that didn't, they took them to these chapels or these centres and then hoped that someone, you know, tried to find a home for them - go round like they collect now for flags, 'Will you have this kiddy?' ... My niece lived with us, she were only a little girl, and this Pamela, she were the same age, so we chose her and she came to live with us.

"... her mum never sent a letter, or 'thank-you' letter, or 'Is she all right?' We could have been horrible people, we could have ill-treated her, we could have been perverts. That little girl's mother, we never heard a word from her and she lived with us for ages, perhaps eighteen months, two years. Her dad came a couple of times on leave, called to see us and came for his tea and she never fussed him, as if she didn't know him.

"... She were a little fat girl, she'd sorta been fed all right but scruffy and dirty, and we'd to clean her hair up and that ... And t'bed, she thought t'bed were lovely, she thought it were a lovely warm bed ... She thought it were lovely at our house. She'd never had a bath - we couldn't get her out of the bath you know, and we clothed her - she'd no clothes. But she's never got in - you'd have thought she'd have, as she got older, got in touch wouldn't you?"
HECKMONDWIKE WOMAN BORN 1926

OLD MAID: "IF THERE'S A WAR I'M GOING TO HAVE SIX CHILDREN!"

BILLETING OF CHILDREN

A "BAMFORTH" COMIC

Evacuees Learn the Dialect.

Some few weeks ago, evacuees, with their cockney accent, invaded the borough and schools. Last week, a teacher had to enquire of a couple of them as to what the boisterous game was they were playing, and they replied: "We are nobbut laiking at Rally-Ho!"

"My brother was in the Air Force and I'd gone into nursing which left two bedrooms free, so we had to have refugees from Jersey. We had a mother and a little girl who was a polio victim and then they were eventually provided with a house ... and then we had a boy who came. We always had a refugee in the house."
HUDDERSFIELD WOMAN BORN 1915

"They came round to see if we could take some boys from Dunkirk, and we had two young men straight from the trenches from Dunkirk."
DEWSBURY WOMAN BORN 1897

"They came round to see if you'd any rooms for evacuees. Well, I had plenty of room so I took a couple in from London with two little children. They stayed with me a while and then after that, when they went, I had a couple in from Sheffield. They had a baby. He was in munitions. And then after that I had a couple in from Edinburgh - oh, and I'd a couple in from Devon as well."
HUDDERSFIELD WOMAN BORN 1916

EVACUEES

When cities suffered severe bombing, those whose homes were destroyed were often evacuated to 'safe' areas for immediate emergency aid. Here two local women talk of their involvement with people who had suffered the bombing of London and Sheffield.

"... they'd been bombing Sheffield, and we were expecting two coach loads - people coming who'd been bombed out. Well, the biggest place was our chapel ... we filled the boilers with water and got a lot of broth going and we got all the bedding we could draw from every resource possible. And we gathered up all the clothing, people were giving us stuff all round. Because they were bombed out with nothing on some of them, just their nightwear ... some of them from very, very poor circumstances, extremely poor, in fact some very degraded families ... some of them were so filthy. There were women with babies, and we'd give them some nappies for the babies and the dirty ones were taken off and when you weren't looking they were throwing them behind the heating pipes and slinging them behind the seats in the chapel, anywhere - filthy! And letting the children do anything around. Well, I, being a sort of controlled person would say 'You can't do that, you must pick that up ... Miss ... who was our leading light said to me 'Oh nurse, you mustn't be rough on these people, they've had a terrible time. They're still in shock you know'. I says 'Well does that mean that we can have typhoid and diseases because they're in shock?'

"... there were a couple of old ladies who've always stayed in my mind. They were really poor but very, very respectable and intelligent people ... and one of them said 'When you've thought the world of your home and had everything in that home just as you wanted it and kept it so spick and span, to be bombed out like this make you realise that it doesn't matter at all as long as you're comfortable ... always remember that your life is much more important than anything material' she said, 'it's taught us that if it's taught us nothing else' ... and they were the only two of that crowd who were what you would call highly respectable people. The rest were the real rough people of Sheffield."

HIGHTOWN WOMAN BORN 1919
NURSE

"You'll like it here - it's so safe" (BUT EVEN 'SAFETY AREAS' SWARM WITH DANGEROUS GERMS)

What a warm-hearted welcome the weary evacuees receive from their hostess in the country. But even in the safe areas there is still danger. Here, too, are enemies that threaten us—dangerous germs. Invisible—they thrive in these overcrowded conditions. They are a threat to us all, day and night, in country and in town. You must protect yourself and everyone in your house from this menace. Scrub every corner with Bodyguard Soap. Its healthy, antiseptic lather will remove every speck of dirt, and so get rid of germs which breed there too.

USE **BODYGUARD**
THE SOAP TO BEAT THOSE GERMS
BG 64A-837

"... my front door bell rang ten o'clock at night, I went to t'door, who should be there but this lad - this soldier from London - and his wife. She was nineteen, expecting a baby any minute, would I take her in? 'Well' I says 'I think you'd better go to t'vicar and see if he can find you room'. 'Oh Mrs ... I wish you'd take her in, will you take her in. I'm going to India and I can't leave her at home'. And she'd been sleeping on t'embankment and she'd been sleeping in t'shelters, in t'underground, and she'd nothing but what she stood up in, not a night-gown. 'Oh' I thought, 'poor thing' ...

"Anyway, cutting t'story short she had this baby, he left her with me. I tried every hospital round here, Staincliffe, Batley, North Bierley, every hospital round Bradford, Leeds to get her in to have that baby and nobody 'd take her because they were full o' soldiers. So I says, 'Well Nelly, there's only one thing for it, you'll have to have it here' ...

"Mrs Roberts next door brings t'hot water and puts it at t'top o' t'stairs in a bowl. I gets all t'towels out what I could find and a night-gown for her. I spread all papers all over t'bed and just as t'baby's head were being born t'nurse came. She comes bouncing upstairs, nearly goes into t'bowl o' water. 'Oh', she says 'the heads been born!'. I says 'Aye I know. You can take over now' I says, 'I've had enough'."

LIVERSEDGE WOMAN BORN 1910

KEEP SMILING THROUGH

The people of Kirklees made the most of their leisure time even though that meant 'going out' in the black-out. Probably the most popular form of entertainment during the war was the cinema - there were scores in the Kirklees area. These were closed down at the beginning of the war together with theatres and dance-halls, but they all soon re-opened. Everyone listened to the radio, and programmes such as ITMA were national favourites - many local people can still recount the characters and their catchphrases! Morale was raised by Forces request programmes which united loved ones separated by the war. Patriotic and sentimental songs flooded out. ENSA organised entertainment in the factories for local workers and all around the area people made their own entertainment.

"... people visited a lot. We used to go visiting often. They'd say 'Go get ready and we'll go and see Mrs So-and-so', 'cause their husbands were in the Forces so t'wives were left on their own. They'd no money so they used to visit a lot. I can remember going to lots of people's houses."
HECKMONDWIKE WOMAN BORN 1926

"... there was I would think about half a dozen cinemas in Batley, Batley Carr and Dewsbury ... there was always plenty on and also the cinema was cheap ... You'd see two main feature films and in between with the adverts you'd have the community singing where they'd put up on the screen the words of 'Run Rabbit' or something like this and everybody would join in singing ..."
HUDDERSFIELD MAN BORN 1931

"I remember when we used to go [to the cinema] in the war there was a lot of prisoners of war you know in the first few rows, and then there would be a space and some more rows, and then we could sit. And we all had to be sitting down, they didn't bring them in till everybody was sitting down."
HUDDERSFIELD WOMAN BORN 1931

"We could go dancing every night, there were always somewhere with a dance, lot more than you have to do now, we'd always something to do. We'd a fabulous time during the war us teenagers."
HECKMONDWIKE WOMAN BORN 1926

"Cambridge Road baths, they put the floor down over the baths and that was one of the favourite places where the big bands came ... Oscar Rabin and Joe Loss ... and then we had the Squadronaires which was a very famous band during the war. And when these really good bands were there ... we danced and then we all stood round the stage and - like you see them now, these pop groups, I suppose in a way it was like that but we weren't so outrageous - but we all stood around and clapped and enjoyed them. It was always packed when we had the big bands - it was lovely!"
HUDDERSFIELD WOMAN BORN 1922

Advertisement for the Ritz
Cinema, Huddersfield, 1943.

KEEP SMILING THROUGH

"... they had a lot of troops at this pub in Slaithwaite and they opened a barracks there and we could go there to dance to Slaithwaite barracks. And they had some decent bands there, and I think they had one of their own bands on the premises ... if he [husband] was home on leave from the RAF we would go ... I can't remember us going without being escorted there. But in Huddersfield we could, and some of the local bands there worked at David Brown's. Eric Pearson who was very famous at that time, he played locally and he worked at Brown's, and he used to play in the Co-op Hall ... and it was very nice there. And then Greenhead Masonic, occasionally we went there on Saturdays, and the Town Hall - sometimes they would have a band."
HUDDERSFIELD WOMAN BORN 1922

This Jitterbug Madness.

One of the main pastimes of youth nowadays is dancing; perhaps it always has been, but in Dewsbury, at the Town Hall at any rate, it is in danger of being prohibited. The reason for this, is that to quote from an article in "Youth," the magazine of the Co-operative Youth Club—" In the last few months, I have attended quite a few dances in the Town Hall," says the writer, "and have been appalled at the sight of couples, who, when the band is playing a particularly 'hot' number, retreat into a corner, and then proceed to throw themselves about, twisting and writhing their bodies, and with maniacal grins on their faces, perform antics that would turn a monkey green with envy. And this," he says, "is what they proudly call 'jitterbug' dancing." The writer goes on to say, "Besides making fools of themselves, these jitterbug mad people are a nuisance to other would-be dancers."

How true that article is, the writer of this knows from his own personal experience what it is to be kicked, butted and tripped up while vainly striving to keep his feet and attempting to dance.

Brighten your Black-Out With Radio

In these times of emergency radio is absolutely essential. It is also the chief means by which the public will receive the latest news and instructions by Radio Communication.

THORNES ARE WELL STOCKED WITH A LARGE CHOICE OF ALL THE BEST IN RADIO.

...r your A.R.P. SHELTER or Refuge Room we ...e PORTABLE BATTERY or ELECTRIC SETS n £4-19-6.

...al purchase of A.R.P. LANTERNS, complete Batteries, 3/- each.

...f all makes and types of Radio immediately.

S W. THORNES LIMITED
RGATE, BURY ...sbury
2, COMMERCIAL ST., BATLEY
'Phone 750 Batley

"We did have 'Workers Playtime' - they used to have it on the radio all the time. And when they [ENSA] were coming they came into the canteen, and I didn't go home to dinner that day, we all stopped ... I don't think it was anybody really famous, but we had a good sing and there was a comedian and all sorts."
HUDDERSFIELD WOMAN BORN 1922
MUNITIONS WORKER, DAVID BROWN'S

"There were all the fairs - they shut 'em all up at the beginning, they got scaredy at t'beginning and shut 'em all up and then gradually they allowed 'em to open provided they blacked all out. And what they used to do, they used to run dark covers all t'way round and a minimum of lighting, and they let 'em carry on running. And of course t'pictures used to open just same as normal. You could go to t'pictures same as normal. I mean, well, it wouldn't have done to shut everything up would it. I mean folks spirits 'd have gone to t'floor, flat. It were bad enough as it was."
ROBERTTOWN MAN BORN 1912

"My husband's a pianist and [in the evenings] we sung, we had a lot of music. We loved the radio, we loved to listen to a play on the radio and get sat up to the fire, really enjoy the radio play and some of the radio programmes such as ITMA and things like that, music programmes. And we used to get tickets from the hospital, from patients who'd been in, grateful patients gave us tickets to go up to Bradford Alhambra or to the Princess Theatre and we saw some wonderful shows."
HIGHTOWN WOMAN BORN 1919
NURSE

"There were two channels on the radio - there was the Home Service and the Forces Programme. We had people like Vera Lynn who did a very fine job in singing nostalgic songs about yearning wives and girlfriends and so forth ... For morale through the war it did a magnificent job. It cheered everyone up. There were lots of comedy programmes, and there were people in these programmes who became national figures ... ITMA ran all the way through the war and indeed till after the war and I think it did a marvellous thing in keeping up the morale ... a lot of the catchphrases became used by the public, everybody would use these ... People getting on buses would say, you know, 'After you, Cecil,' and I think that, silly as it sounds these days, these things helped morale ..."
BATLEY MAN BORN 1926

" 'Hanging out the Washing on the Siegfried Line' - Oh, what was all those old ones - oh 'White Cliffs of Dover' and all them were popular, and Vera Lynn was very popular on a Sunday night, we used to listen to her. And then used to be 'Lili Marleen' - that was a German one wasn't it? - they used to sing that a lot."
WILSHAW WOMAN BORN 1905

HOLIDAYS AT HOME?

To reduce non-essential use of public transport, the 'Holidays at Home' scheme was designed in 1941 to encourage people not to travel away for their holidays by providing large scale programmes of entertainment at home during the summer. It was very successful and local people were delighted with the great variety of entertainment so easily and frequently available in their local parks. Huddersfield claimed to be the 'pioneers' of the 'Holidays at Home' movement. Holidays to the coast did continue for some, but many local people were content to give up travelling for the duration of the war. The scheme was also a great bonus to those who could not afford holidays anyway under normal circumstances.

Town Ales Brewery advertisement. The brewery at Lockwood has since closed.

'Holidays at Home' Programme of entertainment at Greenhead Park, Huddersfield.

"... there was no such thing as thinking 'I'm going to pack up and I'll get off to Southport for a week' or anything like that. That wasn't on, because most of the people at Southport or these seaside places were billeting soldiers who were under training or something like that. Travel was very restricted - you couldn't sort of catch a train anywhere you wanted at any time, and also there always seemed to be that threat about that if anything happened to the family ... you always thought that you wanted to stick together. There was no pleasure in leaving the family behind for any length of time."
NEW MILL MAN BORN 1920

"We were told in the summer that in the national interest we should stay away from the coast. In any case the seaside areas were sort of blanked off with barbed wire and so forth. Some of them were mined, and so it was useless anyway, and we were encouraged to have holidays at home. And as a result there were all kinds of junketings went on at the various parks. I remember all kinds of things going on at Batley Park, Dewsbury Crow Nest Park and so forth to try to make everybody happy and give a sort of festive feeling."
BATLEY MAN BORN 1926

HOLIDAYS AT HOME?

"The 'Holidays at Home' were very well patronized. They were held in the majority in Greenhead Park and they ran all through the school holidays ... with a very comprehensive programme. They'd have talent contests, they'd theatre. They'd have events on in the main arena and the highlight of that for me was the gymkhana, and they'd show-jumping there ... and they used to have motorcycle displays, the Royal Corps of Signals came with their display team. They'd pet shows, they'd brass band contests. They'd all kinds of things. And it proved very popular. People couldn't go away and they had something in the park, something very close and cheap because it was just something in the bag for the band and that was about all it cost you. It was good, very well run organisation."
GOLCAR MAN BORN 1922

"Monday it was the dancing, Miss France's dancing kids; and on Tuesday there was a bit of a comedy, I think it was just anybody went and did something; and then on a Wednesday there was a proper concert party and the band leaders, they used to play; then on the Thursday it was the childrens talent spotting; and then on Friday, there wasn't anything on a Friday, not in the tent; then on the Saturday it would be the finals for the week for the children who'd got through to the top and that's how it went all the week through. Then there would be the dance evenings - three nights a week there was a dance. Every night there was something. Every afternoon and every night there was something going on - Punch and Judy shows and all sorts of things in the concert place."
HUDDERSFIELD WOMAN BORN 1902
'HOLIDAYS AT HOME' ORGANISER

Local people on holiday in Morecambe towards the end of the war.

"That old lady ... she was always the first there. Every concert she was on the front row and this particular day it bolted down, it rained and rained and rained and she was still there and we kept saying 'You want to go home, there'll be no concert today!' Anyway the concert party took pity on her and they'd give her a special concert all to herself, she had it all to herself and then somebody gave her a bouquet of flowers. She was a really staunch 'Holiday at Home' person."
HUDDERSFIELD WOMAN BORN 1902
'HOLIDAYS AT HOME' ORGANISER

"We, as a family, I don't think we missed going to Scarborough once the whole of the war ... I can remember we used to be on the front, and of course it was all barbed wire on the front at Scarborough ... you could see the smoke of the convoys going up and down the North Sea and periodically you could hear gunfire as they were being bombed by aircraft."
GOMERSAL MAN BORN 1928

"We could always have a few days over in Blackpool y'know. We didn't go anywhere else, it was just because it was handy and you could go to all the shows."
HUDDERSFIELD WOMAN BORN 1899

CHRISTMAS IN WARTIME

Local people did not let war prevent them from celebrating Christmas in the traditional way. A little ingenuity, patience and sharing could usually ensure something a bit special. Absent loved ones were never far from the thoughts of those at home, who treasured communications received from them, especially at family times such as Christmas. Local War Comforts Funds sent out Christmas parcels to servicemen and women from their own towns. For example in 1941 Batley sent 3,000 parcels, most of them packed and despatched by Fox's Biscuits. The contents included chocolates, brandy snap, biscuits and cake, as well as packets of liquorice sticks. Such parcels appear to have had a strong morale value, and the local press published columns of appreciative letters from those receiving them.

Two Forces Christmas greetings sent by a local man serving in the Middle East to his fiancée from Mirfield, serving in the ATS.

Gunner Frank Robinson, R.A.—I could not have wished for anything better when I saw a packet of ginger biscuits, which is my favourite.

A.C.2 J. Carter, R.A.F.—If every town did the same to its serving sons and daughters as Batley does, I am sure things would seem easier. My pals said what a lucky bloke I was, so I told them that Batley was the best place on the map.

Corpl. Constance M. Talbot, R.A.—It is always an event in the Army to receive a parcel from home, and one from so many citizens of my home town gave me a great deal of pleasure. Batley has a flair for doing things properly, and I assure you that this parcel is no exception.

Extracts printed in *The Batley News* from appreciative letters sent by local servicemen and women about Christmas parcels they had received from the people of Batley and Birstall.

"Christmas - weil you made an effort. You saved your rations. You put things in store for the time and if you got something a bit of a treat like some candied peel, that was treasured, and my mother would go to some effort to make a Christmas cake and Christmas pudding. But they were celebrated, don't worry, they were celebrated!"
GOLCAR MAN BORN 1922

CHRISTMAS IN WARTIME

"... I always remember the first year of the war, sweets weren't rationed then, it hadn't come to that, and so my job - although like I say, I was only nine that first Christmas - to enable us to have a few sweets to eat at Christmas my morning jobs, Saturday mornings, was going into town with a big brown carrier bag and some money and rushing round, 'cause each different confectioners had a supply of sweets and I don't quite know how they were released, but I remember queueing and running from shop to shop to get just a few things that you were allocated ... You could have maybe two Fry's bars or something else and then you'd run to another shop and get something else. So with doing that, you see, by the time Christmas came this carrier bag was quite full.'
DEWSBURY WOMAN BORN 1930

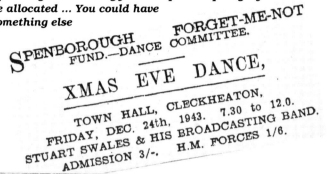

"When we couldn't get a turkey we got three shillings worth of pork, shoulder pork, and that was all we got. And then I used to make pies, big plate pies with the sausagemeat we got from America ... Actually we did very well at Christmas, but one time the butcher had promised to get us a turkey and when I went down to see about it he said he couldn't get any at all and that was on the Christmas Eve. So I'd to go for my husband, and there was a fish shop, and I happened to know him, and we told him about it and we managed to get a turkey from him, otherwise we wouldn't have had any meat."
HUDDERSFIELD WOMAN BORN 1899

CHRISTMAS CAKES
MUST BE ORDERED

Owing to the War-Time Rationing there is a scarcity of the Dried Fruits, Peels and Spices which go to make a real Christmas Cake. We shall give as good a Service as possible.

HELP US BY ORDERING AT ONCE YOUR REQUIREMENTS FOR CHRISTMAS PUDDINGS. CAKES, MINCEMEAT, FANCIES and STAND-PIES

MISSES

M. & C. SHACKLETON
HICK LANE JUNCTION, BATLEY.
Telephone 279

"We were supposed to be going to stay with him [grandfather in Manchester] for Christmas because it was the first Christmas he was on his own, and he'd invited us. Well, when we got to Manchester there'd been an air raid and no trains were going through so we had to turn back. So immediately me father sent a telegram to say that we couldn't get through, and the telegram never arrived. And one of the neighbours told us after that he was standing at the door - and he always used to wear a big white apron - for hours looking up the road, waiting and wondering. He'd made a meat and potato pie for us Christmas dinner and he was waiting there for us to turn up ..."
HUDDERSFIELD WOMAN BORN 1925

"I remember making a list for Father Christmas and being slightly disappointed if I didn't get the main thing that was on it. But it was wartime and it was terribly difficult to get something and so for instance if we asked for a desk we might get a book or something like that, something slightly different. But they were hard times and things were just not available in those days."
HUDDERSFIELD WOMAN BORN 1939

"I always made Christmas cake and Christmas pud' 'cause there again there were wartime recipes with not a lot of stuff in, not as many ingredients ... they seemed to bring a few things out at Christmas, y'know dried fruit and that sort of thing so that you had a little bit to do something with. But you couldn't be making the rich fruit cakes and puddings of old ... but everybody did their best."
HUDDERSFIELD WOMAN BORN 1915

"Quite often they were made presents. You know a home-made calender was acceptable. Flower arrangements and things like that. Anything you could get a bit out of the ordinary."
GOLCAR MAN BORN 1922

GETTING MARRIED

In common with all other aspects of life wedding celebrations were affected by the war. Hurried weddings and shortages of clothing coupons often meant that couples dispensed with traditional white, and many were married in uniform. Limited food supplies could cause problems at the wedding reception - it was a time when family and friends rallied round to make as grand a celebration as possible with what was available.

"... mostly they wore their uniform to save coupons because if they were going to start to have to make a wedding out of the material they got with the coupons it'd cost a lot of money, and they wouldn't be able to save up coupons."
LIVERSEDGE WOMAN BORN 1910

"On the twenty-third of December I was getting married, and so I came home on the twenty-second - the day before! Well, you know, we didn't have any coupons, you see, and at that time you could borrow a wedding dress from the Forces, and so I did that - I borrowed this wedding dress ... it was rather nice. It was satin with a gathered neck and of course full length. I had a choice of three actually when I went to get this dress ... got to the station at Euston to come home the day before the wedding. Well of course the train was packed from end to end - just standing, and all the corridors, all the doorways were crowded with people. And I'm frantically running up the platform, you know, trying to find a way in, and just about time for the train to set off, and I'm knocking and saying 'Please let me in, I'm getting married tomorrow. I've got to get home today!' So some soldiers very kindly opened the door and let me crowd in with them, you know - course, I had to stand nearly all the way!"
HUDDERSFIELD WOMAN BORN 1923
WREN

"You'd to make your own [wedding]. I'd to borrow a dress and my mother did the flowers for me - we had some white chrysanthemums in the garden - 'cause you couldn't afford to do much else y'know. And my mother made my bouquet - I always remember three large chrysanthemums at either side with a big bow trailing down. And my sister wore a dance dress, a pink taffeta dance dress - you had to do things like that ... my brother was home on leave and he gave me away. That was in 1940 ... even the photographer y'know, all he could allow was about six or seven photographs ..."
BIRSTALL WOMAN BORN 1917

"We had our reception at the Co-op cafe ... we wanted to get it all over with by about five o'clock because it was coming dark y'see at that time and everybody wanted to get home before the sirens started again."
HUDDERSFIELD WOMAN BORN 1915

"If you were catering the wedding yourself people would give you things. You'd save up your currants, your raisins whatever. Someone 'd give you some sugar. Some more 'd give you some of their margarine ration. People were very good y'know that way - they'd give, contribute to it."
HUDDERSFIELD WOMAN BORN 1925

A local wedding, 1942, with the groom in uniform.

"I remember I had a two tier wedding cake but one tier was just a piece of cardboard iced over because there weren't enough ingredients for two cakes. So I had a cake at the bottom but the top cake was just sort of - it looked like a wedding cake you know but there was nothing inside ..."
HUDDERSFIELD WOMAN BORN 1923

RELATIONSHIPS

For many local people war meant separation from their loved ones and great upheavals in family life. Although most people accepted this as a fact of war, separation was still unpleasant. Frequent written communications between home and abroad were maintained, even though censored, but for those women whose men were away fighting, there was still the continual waiting for news, the worrying, and the uncertainty.

"Well of course everybody were down in t'dumps. We didn't know what were going to happen. You didn't know how long they'd be - you didn't know what were going to happen! He did get into t'Air Force which he wanted ..."
LIVERSEDGE WOMAN BORN 1910

"He was in the anti-aircraft. He went in 1941 and course he didn't come back till it was over. He went all up Italy ... I never saw him for, oh I don't know, three or four years ... he just came once, nearly at the end, and then he had to go back. Oh they were difficult days you know, difficult days."
HUDDERSFIELD WOMAN BORN 1909

"He was in Egypt. He came home from Egypt about a month before we were married ... I used to write a letter every night - every night! When he came home he had a great big pile of letters."
HUDDERSFIELD WOMAN BORN 1923

"... my hair went white at the front! I did worry. Because sometimes there was a long time in between that you never heard anything you know. Actually it went quite white in the front - I had golden hair at the time!"
HUDDERSFIELD WOMAN BORN 1899

"He was a very, very lucky man was my husband. I thank God many a time for this because he went in A1 as they called it and a very fit man. He came out A1 ... He was kept in this country until the last twelve months of the war, and then all these soldiers that had been kept over here doing a vital job were sent over there to release the fighting men ... I wasn't really upset because the war was more or less over ... so I really counted my blessings because if he'd have gone at the beginning I think I would have been heartbroken ... it's a big upheaval out of somebody's life."
BIRSTALL WOMAN BORN 1917

"... all the men had been called up and therefore there were nobody to wed. Those that were courtin', their boyfriends were called up and they had to wait for 'em coming back - if they came back!"
LIVERSEDGE WOMAN BORN 1910

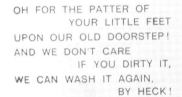

OH FOR THE PATTER OF
        YOUR LITTLE FEET
UPON OUR OLD DOORSTEP!
AND WE DON'T CARE
        IF YOU DIRTY IT,
WE CAN WASH IT AGAIN,
        BY HECK!

RELATIONSHIPS

Immediately war was declared many people rushed to get married. The hurried wartime marriage continued to be commonplace as men and women faced long separation. Local people have also revealed some of the difficulties the demands of war service could cause for those planning their weddings.

"Me sister, she got married. She were in the ATS, and he got t'special licence - they used to get married like that. I mean she'd courted him for years. And she got married in the uniform. He came home on the Friday, he says 'I've got five days leave'. They went an' got this special licence and they'd to go to Wakefield, to the Bishop of Wakefield. And they got married at Heckmondwike Parish Church ... she got married in her uniform, and we haven't even got a photograph of her at all."
HECKMONDWIKE WOMAN BORN 1926

"We were married at Christmas and he was called up in the January ... and we had a fortnight - I was allowed a fortnight to get married and honeymoon, and I remember sending a telegram asking if I could have a bit longer because I wasn't very well. Wasn't true, I was all right. But no, I got a telegram back saying you know, 'Report such and such a time, such and such a place, such and such a date' so I had to go, and then about a fortnight later [he] was called up. So he was just more or less going in as I was just coming out ..."
HUDDERSFIELD WOMAN BORN 1923
WREN

"When we were married y'see [he] was in the Fire Service and he asked for a day off to be married, and he didn't get it so he just took it! But about five days before, he was taken off. Huddersfield firemen, a lot of them were sent off ... so [he] was in Manchester - and you didn't know where they were. They reported for duty y'see - he was up at Lindley - well, they were just sent off! You'd no idea where they were or how long they were going to be. Well I'd visions of not having a bridegroom! But anyway he came back with about four days beard the day before, so we did manage to get married ... the day after we were married we went to our little house, and then the day after, I was back at home with my mum and dad 'cause they didn't fancy me being by myself, and he was back at Lindley on duty ..."
HUDDERSFIELD WOMAN BORN 1915

"We got married first of all. As soon as war was declared we thought we ought to get married. We'd planned to get married later on, but we got married by special licence."
HOLMFIRTH MAN BORN 1910

"I got married in 1940. He came home on embarkation leave and we were married. He went back on t'Tuesday and I never saw him for four and three-quarter years. So during that time you see I were half single and half married as you might say, but they couldn't really send me away from home [for war work] ... If you didn't have any ties you were supposed to go away from home."
HUDDERSFIELD WOMAN BORN 1918
WAR WORKER, ENGINEERING

FULL BOMBER CREW PRESENT.

◆

INTERESTING ST. MARK'S WEDDING.

When you come home on Leave

"I'LL BE WAITING TO GREET YOU WITH A SMILE AND A TEAR---
I CAN HARDLY BEAR WAITING
TILL THAT HAPPY TIME DRAWS NEAR!"

RELATIONSHIPS

Many local people lost their loved ones in the war, and many understandably prefer to keep their memories and feelings private. For others there were different kinds of ordeals and anguish to face. Some saw their loved ones badly maimed - many returning servicemen had to cope with physical disfigurement or disability at a young age. The terrible experiences suffered in POW camps stayed with some men after the war. Wartime separation could cause strains in marriages, with some husbands or wives finding new partners. Hurried wartime marriages followed by immediate separations meant that some husbands and wives were almost strangers to each other. Illigitimate births were not uncommon - such statistics rose during the war years. Some Kirklees people have talked about their own experiences and those of people they knew.

"I had a cousin who got involved with an Australian soldier, and she was a very very quiet, immature sort of girl, and he went back and told her he would come back for her. And of course he didn't and he was married with three or four children. And she had his baby, and she died having the baby, and that was one tragedy in our sort of war."
CLECKHEATON WOMAN BORN 1932

"My husband were very badly wounded during the war. I didn't know him then but he said you'd be amazed how many blokes that had their ears shot off and their nose and things like that, and their girlfriends came and saw them and didn't come again. I thought that would have been awful if somebody'd have done that to him. And I mean, I met him and he had some scars on his face and he used to think - he were only young and he used to think - 'God I'll never get a nice girl'. And I mean I could have - well, I'd me share of boyfriends sort of thing, and we went to this dance and he kept coming to dance with another two blokes, and he thought 'Oh I haven't a chance with her', you know, 'She won't pick me' and I did! And he'll say many a time 'I never thought you'd choose me when these other blokes came to dance', y'know - 'cause he'd seen so many blokes and t'girls that come and thought 'Oh God', and pack 'em in, you know. Which I suppose it were cruel but when you're young girls, you know, you think 'Oh Lord', you don't want to marry - you go for looks mostly as a rule y'know. But he said he saw a lot of that and he were glad he hadn't a girlfriend."
HECKMONDWIKE WOMAN BORN 1926

DREAMING

I'M DREAMING OF YOU ALL THE TIME,
AND OF FUTURE JOYS TO BE.
OF HAPPY TIMES WE'LL HAVE, DEAR.
WHEN YOU COME BACK TO ME!

"There were a lot of problems because some girls that I knew, when their husbands came back y'know the children didn't accept their fathers and all that sort of business. There were a lot of problems one way or another. Some wives had gone off with other chaps and they came home from the war and their wives weren't there. There were really some sad cases."
HUDDERSFIELD WOMAN BORN 1915

"... for a lot of families it was a big strain - a big strain. Because a lot of the wives and husbands had been separated for years - you know, they'd been in the prisoner of war camps and things like that - and it would be like starting over again for a lot of married couples."
HUDDERSFIELD WOMAN BORN 1924

"They'd meet this bloke, he'd come home on leave and they'd get engaged, get married, and then realise after they didn't know 'em, y'know. There were a lot of divorces really. They think it's only happened now but I know lots of people that got married, they met somebody and got married."
HECKMONDWIKE WOMAN BORN 1926

RELATIONSHIPS

"... one girl that lived here, she went with this bloke for two and a half years, and then she were having a baby and she told him, and he were married ... and she thought, y'know, they'd been courting for two and half years! And he used to come home on leave and spend his leaves with her and - I mean, you didn't live with them in those days but ... even then they got pregnant then did girls. And he were a lovely bloke and everybody liked him, and her parents y'know accepted him as if they were courting. And then when she told him she were pregnant he'd to tell her he were married."
HECKMONDWIKE WOMAN BORN 1926

Never Forgotten

SLEEPING OR AWAKE, WITHIN MY THOUGHTS YOU ALWAYS DWELL, AND WHEREVER YOU MAY BE, I HOPE THAT YOU ARE SAFE AND WELL!

FOUND ANOTHER MAN WITH WIFE.

SOLDIER'S RETURN FROM MIDDLE EAST

A Dewsbury soldier who has been serving in the Middle East arrived home after midnight on May 14th and found a man living in his own house with his wife. The man, he discovered upstairs in his wife's bedroom. The soldier told the man to get out which he did and the soldier's wife did not deny that she had been living with the man for a considerable time.

These were the facts alleged at Dewsbury Borough Court on Tuesday when the soldier applied for a separation order and legal custody of the children on the grounds of his wife's adultery.

For the soldier it was stated that in consequence of information received he obtained leave and authority to return to this country. There were five children of the marriage, their ages ranging from 15 years to six years.

The magistrates granted the soldier a separation order and the legal custody of the children.

"... he [husband] was sent to Canada, and then he finished up from Canada to India. But in the meantime of course he'd met this girl and she were expecting his baby and I thought 'Well, it's only one life - mine, between mine and three - him and her and t'baby,' so I gave him his divorce. I says 'Well you can have one if you want'. Well, of course he'd no money so our solicitor says 'Well, I'm sorry but you'll have to pay for it' he says, 'He's nowt' he says 'and he's going back there to marry her'. I says 'Well, it's three lives to one, so I'll fiddle me own canoe', and I've fiddled me own canoe ever since more or less!

"I was engaged to an American soldier who flew, was a pilot ... We had fun on the camp but we used to get the air raid warnings and there'd come a lump in your throat because you knew that there was a lot going out and wouldn't be coming back ... and then the planes you would hear going away, and all t'planes you would hear coming back, and you'd wait - they'd say such and such has come in, such and such has come in, and then they'd tell you who hadn't come in, who hadn't managed to get back, who had been lost somewhere over Germany - including the boy that I was engaged to ..."
HUDDERSFIELD WOMAN BORN 1924
ARMY NURSE

"And in those days you know, divorce, you couldn't claim anything. I had a table an' a chair, and I couldn't claim a thing! You couldn't claim a thing, and nowadays they get half and half don't they, but not then. Whatever he came for, he got, and there were nowt I could do about it. And I wouldn't have cared but the narking part was that while he were in the Forces, I were saving money for him ... you couldn't send money out o' country i' them days, not when t'war were on ... I didn't need it, I'd a good wage in t'police force, so I put his money that they sent me - they have to give you so much from t'Army, from t'Air Force or whatever - and instead of putting it in my name, I put it in his you see. Well, when he came out and wanted his divorce to go back and marry this girl, he could go an' claim it and I couldn't do a thing about it. He just claimed it and that were it, and there's nowt I could do about it. And there were nowt I could do about t'home, although I'd been keeping it going all that time!"
LIVERSEDGE WOMAN BORN 1910

RELATIONSHIPS

"I think that we hardly believed it was real until we met some of these prisoners of war coming back, and we used to go to the railway station to meet them. They'd come then and talk to the people at the meeting in the Art Gallery in Leeds. And one of them brought black bread that they'd been eating in the prison camp. It was very, very dark brown, full of maggots, bone hard, it was a horrible mass and this was their food for a lot of them - this was in Germany and Italy."

HIGHTOWN WOMAN BORN 1919
SECRETARY, FAR EAST PRISONERS OF WAR
ASSOCIATION, LEEDS

"It was three and a half years before my sister-in-law heard that my brother was a prisoner of war. And he had a most beautiful set of teeth - they knocked all his teeth out because an officer had to take the punishment for the men ... he must have been in a terrible state because when he did eventually come home his stomach was so distended, you just couldn't believe it possible, from being fed after starving for so long."

HIGHTOWN WOMAN BORN 1919
SECRETARY, FAR EAST PRISONERS OF
WAR ASSOCIATION, LEEDS

Not only were husbands and wives and sweethearts forced apart. Families were also broken up when parents lost their sons or daughters to the war - sometimes for ever. For many young people it was their first time away from their homes and families - an adventure for some, but for others it could lead to loneliness and homesickness. Both children and parents suffered when the fathers went off to war and missed several years of their children's young lives. Mothers were left to bring up the family alone, without the emotional and financial support of their husbands.

"Oh it were awful, we were crying all over the place, we thought it was awful - me brother-in-law got wounded in Italy, and me brother was haemophiliac and we didn't think he ought to go, but they passed him, so that were a worry. Me mum used to worry herself sick, and especially when they made him into a sniper, he must have been good with a rifle, perhaps. He was about, what, twenty-two, twenty-three and good with a rifle so they made him into a sniper. Well, that's last job he should have had is being a sniper, being a haemophiliac!"

HECKMONDWIKE WOMAN BORN 1926

GOOD-BYE, DADDY! GOD BLESS!

"There was a neighbour just across the way who had a son of my age and he went into the Navy, and on his first run out he was on the Russian convoys - which were hell! - and he was lost on the first convoy. And I remember well the neighbour coming into our house and all the terrible sadness, how upset. My mother tried to comfort her. Her only son - he was gone, just like that. And I remember too at this time it was just before I was called up and I was expecting to go in the Air Force and I remember my mother and father, y'know, their faces got longer and longer as the time came for my call up."

BATLEY MAN BORN 1926

PUBLIC NOTICES.

BATLEY PRISONERS OF WAR RELATIVES' ASSOCIATION (Registered under the War Charities Act, 1940).—BRING-AND-BUY SALE in TOWN HALL, BATLEY, TUESDAY, FEBRUARY 15th. Morning 10-30 to 12, Afternoon 2 to 4-30. Admission 1s. For Expenses Fund. 199

RELATIONSHIPS

"... my sister hated the Forces. She was in the ATS - she absolutely hated it! She were homesick because we had a close family and on a Sunday we all used to go - me mum used to say 'She's stationed at York' - and we used to go and take sandwiches because she were homesick. She hated it because she'd never been away from home y'know ... and she thought it were awful that she didn't see us all y'know. We'd quarrel all t'time she was here y'know, she'd hit us because we were younger than her but ... she couldn't bear not to see us all for a week!"
HECKMONDWIKE WOMAN BORN 1926

"Mother used to write every week and when it got bad during the bombing she got quite worried about me and she gave me a pack of stamped addressed cards and said, 'Look, if you haven't got time to write just post a card, you know, each day and I'll know that you are all right,' you know, but I used to write as often as I could."
HUDDERSFIELD WOMAN BORN 1923
WREN

"The only thing that I was unhappy about, he missed the first five years of my daughters life - growing up as a youngster. But some of 'em even missed more than that. I've got a lot to be thankful for."
BIRSTALL WOMAN BORN 1917

"I'm surprised now that I wasn't more worried about my father because ... he was still in France about three weeks after Dunkirk. I mean a lot of people now think that after Dunkirk that was it, the war in Europe was finished. There was a major evacuation from Dunkirk, but there were still a lot of British soldiers getting away - and I don't mean escaping, I mean getting away in large numbers - from places like Cherbourg. And my father came away from Cherbourg I think it would be about three weeks after Dunkirk, spent a short time at home, litle bit of time retraining in Blackpool, and was then sent to Egypt, so he was part of the Eighth Army. And after that he didn't come home until demobilisation, 1945."
HUDDERSFIELD MAN BORN 1931

"... he always used to take me to football. I was very close to my father and he played very serious football as an amateur and he spoiled me as regards football, and then that all suddenly was cut out, and by the time he came back we'd missed something like six years at a very important time. So yes, I missed him, and we never seemed to get back to the same sort of situation that we'd been in before he went ... I would look completely different! He looked the same to me because five years at that age doesn't make a big difference in appearance, but between the ages of sort of eight and fourteen you see a big change in a child."
HUDDERSFIELD MAN BORN 1931

"We were in bed - I don't know what time it was, I think it must have been early morning - and there's stones, little stones [thrown] up at the window. My mum looks out o' the window - 'Oh it's your dad, it's your dad!' Came downstairs ... and she sat me on the table and he put his kit bag down the side. And there was this man there and she just says 'This is your dad'. Well, he didn't mean anything at all to me, he were just a man y'know, but there he was and that were my dad."
GOMERSAL WOMAN BORN 1939

90

RELATIONSHIPS

The war brought suffering even for those without members of their families away on Active Service. War work could bring its own casualties, and many faced great dangers, such as the firemen working away in heavily bombed cities. The realities of war were brought home by the loss or injury of friends, neighbours and colleagues. Some local people have spoken of the friendliness and caring attitudes of the people around them during wartime.

"... we lived near the Co-operative Boot and Shoe Company and they used to have a fire watching team ... I had a friend, and there were three children in that family, and their dad used to go on the roof and fire watch and 'plane spot and what have you, and he fell off and died, and he left his wife with three young children."
HECKMONDWIKE WOMAN BORN 1926

"They [firemen] were in a lot danger, I mean even though they weren't fighting y'know. And blitzes were going on - there were bombs dropping and buildings dropping ... and you did get worried yes, naturally."
HUDDERSFIELD WOMAN BORN 1915
WIFE OF NFS MAN

IT'S ALTERED THINGS, YER KNOW, WITH BOTH MI KIDS EVAPORATED AND MI 'USBAND BUSY IN ONE O' THEM DETERMINATION SQUADS!

"Most of the men was away y'see - I think there would only be about four men up Fanny Moor Lane at home, 'cause they was all off. My husband was one of 'em [at home] and people used to say to me 'Aren't you lucky'. I said 'Why?' She'd say 'Well you've got your husband at home'. I said 'Look, he's at home but he's more in the 'Dye's' [chemical works] than what he's at home'. I never knew when he was coming home! Sometimes he'd go out seven o'clock in the morning to work and probably wouldn't come back till the next morning. I never knew when he was coming home or where he was. It's very rarely he was at home, 'cause if the sirens went he could not come home, he had to stay, so we was left on our own to sort us'selves out y'know."
HUDDERSFIELD WOMAN BORN 1902

"... neither of them came back and I knew them, and I knew their family quite well, and these two, they did have quite an impact on us. You know, rather than seeing that, you know, a hundred airmen hadn't come back from the raid over Germany - that was just a number type of thing, but these were two individuals that we knew."
GOMERSAL MAN BORN 1928

"... more caring towards one another, much more caring. See, somebody always had somebody that was fighting or somebody that was away. I mean if the telegraph boy came down the street, the whole street would be out and the whole street would be sorry with them ..."
HUDDERSFIELD WOMAN BORN 1924

"... there weren't many that went out of the drawing office, but these were two that went earlier, and one of them had both his hands blown off and one of his eyes blown out - and with a grenade ... he was on Active Service but he wasn't in a battlefield, he was showing somebody. And he came back to the drawing office with false arms and he had all his equipment made - with his T-square and his set square - all had sandpaper glued on so he could get a grip on them you know, and he did quite well."
GOMERSAL MAN BORN 1928

"I can only say that I enjoyed my war because I made so many friends - so much love, so much love about, everybody cared, everybody wanted to give."
HUDDERSFIELD WOMAN BORN 1924

THE FINAL DAYS ...

VE Day on 8 May 1945 and VJ Day on 14 August 1945 brought joy and celebrations around Kirklees, as local people held parties, sang and danced in the streets, and thousands flocked into town and village centres. For many though, the joy was tempered with an awareness that life would never be the same again. Although Kirklees had escaped major bombing, death and destruction, many of its servicemen were dead or injured. Now also came realisation that it was time to face up to problems such as broken marriages and disabilities. Others waited impatiently for their loved ones to return from the Forces or prisoner of war camps. Everyone had to rebuild their lives which had been so dramatically altered by the war. For the time being though, most people were simply overjoyed to hear of its end.

Local street party group with 'V for Victory' cake, Thomas Street, Heckmondwike, 1945.

"... at VE Day we all went into Heckmondwike ... and everybody were there and there were a band playing - it were great ... I mean, my mum weren't one for doing owt like that - my mum, dad and all of us were in Heckmondwike and singing and dancing and like they do in London."
HECKMONDWIKE WOMAN BORN 1926

"On VE night I remember we went to town, went and had a few drinks, walked up to Greenhead Park - we were dancing up to Greenhead Park ... everybody was in high spirits and they were all dancing, linking arms, kissing one another, and it seemed to go on for hours. So when we got VJ night we did it again. Had a good time. Everybody did because it was over. You couldn't believe the feeling that it was over. Things could get back to normal. What is normal?"
HUDDERSFIELD MAN BORN 1922

"We went down Cleckheaton - they had a Victory dance at the Town Hall but you couldn't get in. And the square outside, all 'round what was Fox's Cafe before it is as it is today - that area was an absolute seething mass of people."
GOMERSAL MAN BORN 1928

"... this chap that lived just across, Mr Pottinger ... he got his piano and they wheeled it down and ... all the street was dressed up. And Mrs Evans, there was Mrs Bull - everybody! And next to us was Mr Mellor, and everybody brought their table out, and the chairs, and they put them all together, and the cloths, and - oh the piano was going. I can remember that day, oh it was lovely! ... they all brought their stuff out. Oh, it was lovely! And there was dancing and everything. And I can remember my friend Beryl Evans and her brother Rex, they just lived on our street, their dad came home from the Air Force that day. And I remember his mum shouting 'Ooh it's Roy, ooh it's Roy' and everybody went mad you know. And also I remember my friend Jean - I remember her dad coming home from the Army and his wife ran right down the street when she saw him, everybody told her, you know. It's sad when you come to think isn't it? And oh it was fantastic that day - oh it was real!"
HUDDERSFIELD WOMAN BORN 1931

"When the war ended we had a big party in the village. Everybody gathered together and collected tablecloths, knives and forks, spoons, plates, cups and saucers and we had it in the school. Then we had a big party in the street for the kids. Then it was a case of saying 'Who's got my so and so?', and we was all going round searching for all our belongings y'know - it was funny."
HUDDERSFIELD WOMAN BORN 1902

THE FINAL DAYS ...

"I think VE was the time that strikes you most of all, although we were waiting for VJ because my wife had a brother who was a prisoner of war, in Java actually, and you know, we were waiting for news of him."
HIGHTOWN MAN BORN 1920

"... it was wonderful to know that it was all over, but you were sorry for all the people that had been lost, there was a lot from Huddersfield you know that went and were killed and maimed."
HUDDERSFIELD WOMAN BORN 1899

"Somebody flew into the ward and shouted 'The war's over' and even the poor old soldiers sat up in bed and shouts 'Hip, hip, hurray!'. That was the one and only time I was drunk, and I honestly didn't know I was getting drunk. I had a glass of cider and I felt fine until I actually got outside. I slept in a field all night that night ... Oh, it's [celebrations] undescribable really. I mean, sheets and blankets all went to pot in the ward, and we were throwing pillows at one another. Outside, well, all hell was let loose outside ... It had grown tremendously had Catterick ... and I think every camp had come into Catterick centre, and they'd all a drink in their hands so it was - well, it was just marvellous, marvellous! And everybody was singing 'Land of Hope and Glory' and 'There'll Always Be An England' and I think there always will be you know."
HUDDERSFIELD WOMAN BORN 1924
ARMY NURSE

"... we had parties when they came home. All the relatives came and we had parties, yes, it were nice, it were a lovely time - well for some of us, but there were these you see that didn't come home. I mean, my sister-in-law, her brother died. He were only about twenty, and for such as them it's awful if you're having parties and their sons haven't come home."
HECKMONDWIKE WOMAN BORN 1926

"Just before the end [of the war] we came home ... I arrived in the Mersey on the day that Germany packed in, May the eighth 1945, aye. I saw the lights go on in Liverpool when we were stuck in the middle of the damned river. I was away just short of four and a half years out there ... we were stuck on the boat all that night. We saw everything happen [VE celebrations] - and that Mersey ferry was coming across near us - we couldn't do a damned thing, aye. And we gets to shore t'next day, shoved on a train right down to near Southend, and I could have come home from Liverpool in a blooming hour!"
CLECKHEATON MAN BORN 1921
SOLDIER

"I remember going out with my wife, who was then my girlfriend, and standing absolutely fascinated and enraptured at the street lights which had been turned on. We were still fighting the Japanese but we'd obtained Victory in Europe and the street lights were on and it was spring. And there was one particular street light which was shining through the new leaves, this tree with beautiful new greenery and the light diffusing through it. And we stood just watching this, absolutely marvellous to see it after all the dark years."
BATLEY MAN BORN 1926

COME AND HAVE A CUP WITH ME!

"Oh relief and thank goodness, and go to bed to sleep without thinking, no planes going over ... intense relief, you could start to get on with life and live again perhaps, because it was only an existence really. You never knew just what was going to happen, did we?"
HUDDERSFIELD WOMAN BORN 1915

"Jubilant, oh - excited and happy ... dancing in the streets, bunting up, flags everywhere, singing and dancing and oh - jubilation! Yes, it was lovely. Don't want to live through another!"
DEWSBURY WOMAN BORN 1897

... AND AFTER

The effects of the war on local people did not come to an end with the termination of hostilities in 1945. The Second World War took its toll in many different ways - loss or injury of loved ones, strains in marriages, disruption of careers and education - the results of which were not always immediately apparent. The war also opened up new opportunities for many, providing a chance to meet people, see places and have experiences that they would have been unlikely to under normal circumstances. Some local people have spoken of some of the more hidden, often tragic, results and longer lasting effects of the war years on their personal lives.

"After I'd been in the Forces, like a lot more lads, I took a long time adjusting back to civilian life you know. It isn't as easy as people think. In fact my father once had me on his own one night, everybody else was out, and he had a talk to me over this adjustment you know. Now my brother, he adjusted straightaway. He went straight back to work and he adjusted as if he'd never been away. Now I couldn't. I took months and months. I just couldn't adjust at all. So I went back like I said straightaway down to the mill, got my job back. I don't know - it wasn't the same, the atmosphere wasn't the same. I don't know, I just can't put my finger on it, it just wasn't there, what was there when I first started during - you know at the beginning of the war. And of course I'd learned as a soldier to stick up for myself a little bit more and I was a bit older and I'm afraid me and the gaffer didn't get on too well. And he made a crack about us being all alike, 'You blokes who have been in the Forces are all alike', this that and another you know ... implying we were lazy devils, that's what he meant you know and so in basic English I told him where to stick his job, if you know what I mean. So after that I'd no enthusiasm to go seek a job at all."
MIRFIELD MAN BORN 1922
SOLDIER

"I was happy to get back to work. After being back four months I was really fed up of work. I was fed up of the inside, I couldn't settle inside. And another thing which is nothing whatever to do with work, I found sleeping in a proper bed not easy. In fact, my first leave home - I was abroad four years and nine months - and the first leave that I got home I slept my first three nights on the floor-boards in the bedroom, I was more comfortable on a hard surface than a soft one."
HUDDERSFIELD MAN BORN 1914
SOLDIER

"... when I see some of my old friends now we often say it was like our university, you know, it was our experience of life, our university. Yes, in retrospect I wouldn't have missed it because I think it was a great experience, a great leveller of people. Because you met people that you would normally not have met, did things that you would never have done either, and in the days when very few people went away from home, at least you got away from home."
MIRFIELD WOMAN BORN 1923 ATS

"He [brother] did tell us one or two things [about being in a Japanese POW camp] but they were mostly the funnier things ... He didn't want to talk about the other things, but his wife told us that he'd go to sleep on the settee in the day and he'd have the most terrible dreams. He'd be shrieking, and she learned more during his sleep than she learned from him. In the night she'd wake him up and he'd be choking her to death because she'd touched him and he thought it was a Jap., and he suffered terribly. And when he came home we found out that his back was held together with leather straps and dressings from the beating that he'd had. He was a different person completely from the man who went out ... he had a young daughter and she hadn't seen him from being a baby until she was six, and he was dead when she was fourteen. He had to go into hospital and he had one very serious operation and they said he'd have to keep off the drink before they could do another, and I'm afraid he turned to drink with all the suffering he'd had and he died. He was a man who loved life and he hadn't had anything of it at all."
HIGHTOWN WOMAN BORN 1919

"... one of the things that it [war] did to me, I mean it's a small price to have to pay I readily admit, but one of the things that affected me most of all, it broke into my studies and I never got going again properly. Some people did. Some people who'd been in the Forces got special grants, went to universities and took degrees, I've two friends that did. I wasn't eligible ... I hadn't been in the Forces, because Home Guard didn't count you see."
HIGHTOWN MAN BORN 1920
HOME GUARD

Well I think everybody really was genned up thinking there was going to be a better world, yes, I really think so. You were hoping so you know. 'Cause it had been a long war and I suppose those were the things that had kept everybody going ... you had to be optimistic hadn't you. You'd to hope that all these lads had fought for a better world, that's what they'd gone for. But have they? ..."
HUDDERSFIELD WOMAN BORN 1915

BIBLIOGRAPHY

Kirklees Sound Archive
*Oral History Interviews from Wartime,
Childhood and Industry Projects.*

GOVERNMENT PUBLICATIONS 1938-1945, AND OTHER CONTEMPORARY SOURCES

Heath, Ambrose
New Dishes for Old
A & C Black, 1942

Home Office
*Personal Protection Against Gas.
Air Raid Precautions Handbook No 1.*
2nd Edition HMSO, 1938

Home Office
*Anti-Gas Protection of Babies and Young
Children*
HMSO, 1939

Huddersfield Corporation
*Huddersfield Holidays at Home:
Official Souvenir Handbook 1941.*
Parks and Holiday Entertainments
Committee, 1941

Huddersfield Corporation
*Huddersfield Holidays at Home:
Souvenir Programme 1942.*
Parks and Holiday Entertainments
Committee, 1942

Huddersfield Corporation
*Huddersfield Holidays at Home:
Souvenir Handbook 1943.*
Huddersfield 'Holidays At Home' Committee,
1943

Lord Privy Seal's Office
*Some Things You Should Know if War
Should Come:
Public Information Leaflet No. 1.*
HMSO, July 1939

Lord Privy Seal's Office
*Your Gas Mask:
Public Information Leaflet No. 2.*
HMSO, July 1939

Lord Privy Seal's Office
*Evacuation Why and How?
Public Information Leaflet No. 3.*
HMSO, July 1939

Lord Privy Seal's Office
*Your Food in Wartime:
Public Information Leaflet No. 4.*
HMSO, July 1939

Lord Privy Seal's Office
*Fire Precautions in Wartime:
Public Information Leaflet No. 5.*
HMSO, August 1939

Ministry of Food
*War Cookery Leaflet - Making the Fat
Ration Go Further.*
HMSO, 1944

Ministry of Food
General Ration Book.
HMSO, 1942

Ministry of Home Security
*Incendiary Bombs and Fire Precautions:
Air Raid Precautions Handbook No. 9.*
HMSO, 1942

Ministry of Home Security
What To Do About Gas.
HMSO

Ministry of Information
*Manpower - The Story of Britain's
Mobilisation for War.*
HMSO, 1944

Ministry of Labour & National Service
Explanatory Leaflet on the Home Guard.
HMSO

*War Emergency Information and
Instructions.*
HMSO

LOCAL NEWSPAPERS 1939-1945

*The Batley News
The Batley Reporter and Guardian
The Cleckheaton & Spenborough Guardian
The Dewsbury Reporter
The Huddersfield Daily Examiner
The Yorkshire Reporter*

SECONDARY WORKS

Calder, Angus
The People's War
Jonathan Cape Ltd, 1969

Chamberlin, E.R.
Life in Wartime Britain
B T Batsford, 1972

Edwards, Commander K, RN
Operation Neptune
Collins, 1946

Lewis, Peter
A People's War
Methuen, 1986

Longmate, Norman, (ed.)
The Home Front: An Anthology 1938-1945
Chatto & Windus, 1981

Sheridan, Dorothy, (ed.)
*Wartime Women: A Mass-Observation
Anthology*
Heinemann, 1990

Townsend, C. & E.
War Wives: A Second World War Anthology
Grafton Books, 1989

Wicks, Ben
No Time To Wave Goodbye
Bloomsbury, 1988